❧

SHAKESPEARE'S COMEDY

OF

THE WINTER'S TALE

❧

VALLEY IN BOHEMIA.

SHAKESPEARE'S

COMEDY OF

THE WINTER'S TALE.

EDITED, WITH NOTES,

BY

WILLIAM J. ROLFE, LITT. D.,

FORMERLY HEAD MASTER OF THE HIGH SCHOOL, CAMBRIDGE, MASS.

WITH ENGRAVINGS.

NEW YORK ·:· CINCINNATI ·:· CHICAGO

AMERICAN BOOK COMPANY

CONTENTS.

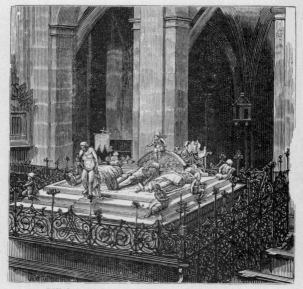

ROYAL MAUSOLEUM IN THE CATHEDRAL AT PRAGUE.

A SEAPORT IN BOHEMIA.
What country, friends, is this? (*T. N.* i. 2. 1).

INTRODUCTION

TO

THE WINTER'S TALE.

I. THE HISTORY OF THE PLAY.

The Winter's Tale, so far as we have any knowledge, was first printed in the folio of 1623, where it is the last of the " Comedies," occupying pages 277 to 303 inclusive.

Malone found a memorandum in the *Office Book* of Sir Henry Herbert, the Master of the Revels, which he gives (see Var. of 1821, vol. iii. p. 229) as follows:

" For the king's players. An olde playe called Winter's Tale, formerly allowed of by Sir George Bucke, and likewyse by mee on Mr. Hemmings his worde that there was nothing profane added or reformed, thogh the allowed booke was missinge, and therefore I returned it without a fee, this 19 of August, 1623."

Malone also discovered that Sir George Buck did not ob-

tain full possession of his office as Master of the Revels until August, 1610 ;* and he therefore conjectured that *The
Winter's Tale* " was originally licensed in the latter part of
that year or the beginning of the next." This date is confirmed by the MS. Diary of Dr. Simon Forman, since discovered (see our ed. of *Richard II.* p. 13, and cf. *M. N. D.*
p. 10), which contains the following reference to the acting
of " the Winters Talle at the glob, 1611, the 15 of maye :" †

" Obserue ther howe Lyontes the kinge of Cicillia was
overcom with Ielosy of his wife, with the kinge of Bohemia,
his frind, that came to see him, and howe he contriued his
death, and wold haue had his cup-berer to haue poisoned,
[*sic*] who gaue the king of bohemia warning ther-of, & fled
with him to bohemia / Remember also howe he sent to the
Orakell of appollo, & the Aunswer of apollo that she was
giltles, and that the king was Ielouse, &c, and howe Except
the child was found Again that was loste, the kinge should
die with-out yssue, for the child was caried into bohemia, &
ther laid in a forrest, & brought vp by a sheppard. And the
kinge of bohemia his sonn maried that wentch, & howe they
fled in Cicillia to Leontes, and the sheppard hauing showed
the letter of the nobleman by whom Leontes sent a [*sic*]
was that child, and the Iewelles found about her. she was
knowen to be leontes daughter, and was then 16 yers old.

Remember also the Rog. that cam in all tottered like
coll pixci / and howe he feyned him sicke & to haue bin
Robbed of all that he had, and how he cosoned the por
man of all his money, and after cam to the shop sher ‡ with
a pedlers packe, & ther cosoned them Again of all ther
money. And howe he changed apparrell with the kinge of

---

* The *Stationers' Registers* show, however, that he had practically the
control of the office from the year 1607.

† We give the passage as printed in the *Transactions of the New Shakspere Society*, 1875–76, p. 416.

‡ That is, sheep-shearing.

THE WINTER'S TALE

DRAMATIS PERSONÆ.

LEONTES, King of Sicilia.
MAMILLIUS, young Prince of Sicilia.
CAMILLO,
ANTIGONUS, } Four Lords of Sicilia.
CLEOMENES.
DION,
POLIXENES, King of Bohemia.
FLORIZEL, Prince of Bohemia.
ARCHIDAMUS, a Lord of Bohemia.
Old Shepherd, reputed father of Perdita.
Clown, his son.
AUTOLYCUS, a rogue.
A Mariner.
A Gaoler.

HERMIONE, Queen to Leontes.
PERDITA, daughter to Leontes and Hermione.
PAULINA, wife to Antigonus.
EMILIA, a lady attending on Hermione.
MOPSA,
DORCAS. } Shepherdesses.

Other Lords and Gentlemen, Ladies, Officers, Guards, Servants, Shepherds, and Shepherdesses.

Time, as Chorus.

SCENE: *Sicilia and Bohemia.*

PORTAL OF PALACE COURT, PRAGUE.

ACT I.

SCENE I. *Antechamber in the Palace of Leontes.*

Enter CAMILLO *and* ARCHIDAMUS.

Archidamus. If you shall chance, Camillo, to visit Bohemia, on the like occasion whereon my services are now on foot, you shall see, as I have said, great difference betwixt our Bohemia and your Sicilia.

Camillo. I think, this coming summer, the King of Sicilia means to pay Bohemia the visitation which he justly owes him.

Archidamus. Wherein our entertainment shall shame us we will be justified in our loves; for indeed—

Camillo. Beseech you,—   10

Archidamus. Verily, I speak it in the freedom of my knowledge; we cannot with such magnificence—in so rare—I know not what to say. We will give you sleepy drinks, that your senses, unintelligent of our insufficience, may, though they cannot praise us, as little accuse us.

Camillo. You pay a great deal too dear for what's given freely.

Archidamus. Believe me, I speak as my understanding instructs me and as mine honesty puts it to utterance.   19

Camillo. Sicilia cannot show himself over-kind to Bohemia. They were trained together in their childhoods; and there rooted betwixt them then such an affection, which cannot choose but branch now. Since their more mature dignities and royal necessities made separation of their society, their encounters, though not personal, hath been royally attorneyed with interchange of gifts, letters, loving embassies; that they have seemed to be together, though absent, shook hands, as over a vast, and embraced, as it were, from the ends of opposed winds. The heavens continue their loves!   30

Archidamus. I think there is not in the world either malice or matter to alter it. You have an unspeakable comfort of your young prince Mamillius; it is a gentleman of the greatest promise that ever came into my note.

Camillo. I very well agree with you in the hopes of him. It is a gallant child; one that indeed physics the subject, makes old hearts fresh: they that went on crutches ere he was born desire yet their life to see him a man.

Archidamus. Would they else be content to die?   39

Camillo. Yes; if there were no other excuse why they should desire to live.

Archidamus. If the king had no son, they would desire to live on crutches till he had one.   [*Exeunt*

SCENE II. *A Room of State in the Same.*

Enter LEONTES, HERMIONE, MAMILLIUS, POLIXENES, CAMIL-LO, *and* Attendants.

Polixenes. <u>Nine changes of the watery star hath been</u>
<u>The shepherd's note since we have left our throne</u>
<u>Without a burthen:</u> time as long again
Would be fill'd up, my brother, with our thanks,
And yet we should, for perpetuity,
Go hence in debt: and therefore, like a cipher,
Yet standing in rich place, I multiply
With one 'We thank you' many thousands moe
That go before it.

Leontes.   Stay your thanks a while;
And pay them when you part.

Polixenes.   Sir, that's to-morrow.   10
I am question'd by my fears, of what may chance
Or breed upon our absence.—That may blow
No sneaping winds at home, to make us say
'This is put forth too truly!'—Besides, I have stay'd
To tire your royalty.

Leontes.   <u>We are tougher, brother,</u>
<u>Than you can put us to 't.</u>

Polixenes.   No longer stay.

Leontes. One seven-night longer.

Polixenes.   Very sooth, to-morrow.

Leontes. We'll part the time between 's then; and in that I'll no gainsaying.

Polixenes.   Press me not, beseech you, so.
There is no tongue that moves, none, none i' the world,   20

So soon as yours could win me; so it should now,
Were there necessity in your request, although
'T were needful I denied it.　My affairs
Do even drag me homeward: which to hinder
Were in your love a whip to me; my stay
To you a charge and trouble: to save both,
Farewell, our brother.

    Leontes.　　　　　Tongue-tied our queen? speak you.

    Hermione. I had thought, sir, to have held my peace until
You had drawn oaths from him not to stay.　You, sir,
Charge him too coldly.　Tell him, you are sure
All in Bohemia's well; this satisfaction
The bygone day proclaim'd: say this to him,
He's beat from his best ward.

    Leontes.　　　　　Well said, Hermione.

    Hermione. To tell, he longs to see his son, were strong:
But let him say so then, and let him go;
But let him swear so, and he shall not stay,
We'll thwack him hence with distaffs.—
Yet of your royal presence I'll adventure
The borrow of a week.　When at Bohemia
You take my lord, I'll give him my commission
To let him there a month behind the gest
Prefix'd for 's parting;—yet, good deed, Leontes,
I love thee not a jar o' the clock behind
What lady she her lord.—You'll stay?

    Polixenes.　　　　　　　　No, madam.

    Hermione. Nay, but you will?

    Polixenes.　　　　　　　I may not, verily.

    Hermione. Verily!
You put me off with limber vows; but I,
Though you would seek to unsphere the stars with oaths,
Should yet say 'Sir, no going.'　Verily,
You shall not go; a lady's 'Verily' is
As potent as a lord's.　Will you go yet?

Hermione is charming — sense of humor which is dangerous
She has sense not to speak where silence is a virtue.

Force me to keep you as a prisoner,
Not like a guest ; so you shall pay your fees
When you depart, and save your thanks.   How say you?
My prisoner? or my guest? by your dread ' Verily,'
One of them you shall be.

   Polixenes.   Your guest, then, madam :
To be your prisoner should import offending ;
Which is for me less easy to commit
Than you to punish.

   Hermione.   Not your gaoler, then,
But your kind hostess.   Come, I 'll question you   60
Of my lord's tricks and yours when you were boys ;
You were pretty lordings then?

   Polixenes.   We were, fair queen,
Two lads that thought there was no more behind
But such a day to-morrow as to-day,
And to be boy eternal.

   Hermione.   Was not my lord
The verier wag o' the two?

   Polixenes. We were as twinn'd lambs that did frisk i' the sun,
And bleat the one at the other.   What we chang'd
Was innocence for innocence ; we knew not
The doctrine of ill-doing, nor dream'd   70
That any did.   Had we pursued that life,
And our weak spirits ne'er been higher rear'd
With stronger blood, we should have answer'd heaven
Boldly ' not guilty ;' the imposition clear'd
Hereditary ours.   nothing but this "original sin"

   Hermione.   By this we gather
You have tripp'd since.

   Polixenes.   O my most sacred lady!
Temptations have since then been born to 's : for
In those unfledg'd days was my wife a girl ;
Your precious self had then not cross'd the eyes
Of my young play-fellow.

Hermione.   <u>Grace to boot!</u>   80
Of this make no conclusion, lest you say
Your queen and I are devils.   Yet go on ;
The offences we have made you do we 'll answer,
If you first sinn'd with us, and that with us
You did continue fault, and that you slipp'd not
With any but with us.
    Leontes.   Is he won yet?
    Hermione. He 'll stay, my lord.
    Leontes.   At my request he would
      not.
Hermione, my dearest, thou never spok'st
To better purpose.
    Hermione.   Never?
    Leontes.   Never, but once.
    Hermione. What! have I twice said well? when was 't
      before?   90
I prithee tell me ; cram 's with praise, and make 's
As fat as tame things : one good deed dying tongueless
Slaughters a thousand waiting upon that.
Our praises are our wages ; you may ride 's
With one soft kiss a thousand furlongs ere
With spur we heat an acre.   But to the goal:
My last good deed was to entreat his stay ;
What was my first? it has an elder sister,
Or I mistake you.   O, would her name were Grace !
But once before I spoke to the purpose ; when?   100
Nay, let me have 't ; I long.
    Leontes.   Why, that was when
Three crabbed months had sour'd themselves to death,
Ere I could make thee open thy white hand
And clap thyself my love ; then didst thou utter
' I am yours for ever.'
    Hermione.   'T is grace indeed.
Why, lo you now, I have spoke to the purpose twice :

The one for ever earn'd a royal husband ;
The other for some while a friend.

 Leontes. [*Aside*]   Too hot, too hot !
To mingle friendship far is mingling bloods.
I have tremor cordis on me : my heart dances ;   110
But not for joy, not joy.   This entertainment
May a free face put on, derive a liberty
From heartiness, from bounty's fertile bosom,
And well become the agent ; 't may, I grant ;
But to be paddling palms and pinching fingers,
As now they are, and making practis'd smiles,
As in a looking-glass, and then to sigh, as 't were
The mort o' the deer,—O, that is entertainment
My bosom likes not, nor my brows !—Mamillius,
Art thou my boy ?

 Mamillius.   Ay, my good lord.

 Leontes.   I' fecks !   120
Why, that 's my bawcock.   What, hast smutch'd thy nose ?—
They say it is a copy out of mine.—Come, captain,
We must be neat ; not neat, but cleanly, captain :
And yet the steer, the heifer, and the calf
Are all call'd neat.—Still virginalling
Upon his palm !—How now, you wanton calf !
Art thou my calf ?

 Mamillius.   Yes, if you will, my lord.

 Leontes. Thou want'st a rough pash and the shoots that I
    have,
To be full like me : yet they say we are
Almost as like as eggs ; women say so,   130
That will say any thing : but were they false
As o'er-dyed blacks, as wind, as waters, false
As dice are to be wish'd by one that fixes
No bourn 'twixt his and mine, yet were it true
To say this boy were like me.   Come, sir page,
Look on me with your welkin eye.   Sweet villain !

Most dear'st! my collop! Can thy dam?—may 't be?—
Affection! thy intention stabs the centre :
Thou dost make possible things not so held,
Communicat'st with dreams ;—how can this be?—   140
With what 's unreal thou coactive art,
And fellow'st nothing. Then 't is very credent
Thou mayst co-join with something ; and thou dost,
And that beyond commission, and I find it,
And that to the infection of my brains
And hardening of my brows.
    Polixenes.   What means Sicilia?
    Hermione. He something seems unsettled.
    Polixenes.   How, my lord!
What cheer? how is 't with you, best brother?
    Hermione.   You look
As if you held a brow of much distraction ;
Are you mov'd, my lord?
    Leontes.   No, in good earnest.—   150
How sometimes nature will betray it's folly,
It's tenderness, and make itself a pastime
To harder bosoms! Looking on the lines
Of my boy's face, methought I did recoil
Twenty-three years, and saw myself unbreech'd,
In my green velvet coat, my dagger muzzled,
Lest it should bite it's master, and so prove,
As ornaments oft do, too dangerous.
How like, methought, I then was to this kernel,
This squash, this gentleman.—Mine honest friend,   160
Will you take eggs for money?
    Mamillius. No, my lord, I 'll fight.
    Leontes. You will! why, happy man be 's dole!—My
        brother,
Are you so fond of your young prince as we
Do seem to be of ours?
    Polixenes.   If at home, sir,

He 's all my exercise, my mirth, my matter,
Now my sworn friend and then mine enemy,
My parasite, my soldier, statesman, all.
He makes a july's day short as December,
And with his varying childness cures in me   170
Thoughts that would thick my blood.

 Leontes.   So stands this squire
Offic'd with me. We two will walk, my lord,
And leave you to your graver steps.—Hermione,
How thou lov'st us, show in our brother's welcome ;
Let what is dear in Sicily be cheap :
Next to thyself and my young rover, he 's
Apparent to my heart.

 Hermione.   If you would seek us,
We are yours i' the garden ; shall 's attend you there ?

 Leontes. To your own bents dispose you ; you 'll be
  found,
Be you beneath the sky.—[*Aside*] I am angling now,   180
Though you perceive me not how I give line.
Go to, go to !
How she holds up the neb, the bill to him !
And arms her with the boldness of a wife
To her allowing husband !

   [*Exeunt Polixenes, Hermione, and Attendants.*
       Gone already !
Inch-thick, knee-deep, o'er head and ears a fork'd one !—
Go, play, boy, play.—Thy mother plays, and I
Play too, but so disgrac'd a part, whose issue
Will hiss me to my grave ; contempt and clamour
Will be my knell.—Go, play, boy, play.—There have been,   190
Or I am much deceiv'd, cuckolds ere now.
Should all despair
That have revolted wives, the tenth of mankind
Would hang themselves. Physic for 't there is none ;
It is a bawdy planet, that will strike

        D

Where 't is predominant : many thousand on 's
Have the disease, and feel 't not.—How now, boy !

   Mamillius. I am like you, they say.

   Leontes.   Why, that 's some comfort.—
What, Camillo there?

   Camillo. Ay, my good lord.   200

   Leontes. Go play, Mamillius ; thou 'rt an honest man.—

                                  [*Exit Mamillius.*

Camillo, this great sir will yet stay longer.

   Camillo. You had much ado to make his anchor hold;
When you cast out, it still came home.

   Leontes.   Didst note it?

   Camillo. He would not stay at your petitions, made
His business more material.

   Leontes.   Didst perceive it?—
[*Aside*] They 're here with me already, whispering, rounding,
' Sicilia is a so-forth ;' 't is far gone,
When I shall gust it last.—How came 't, Camillo,
That he did stay?

   Camillo.   At the good queen's entreaty.   210

   Leontes. At the queen's be 't : ' good ' should be pertinent ;
But, so it is, it is not.   Was this taken
By any understanding pate but thine?
For thy conceit is soaking, will draw in
More than the common blocks ;—not noted, is 't
But of the finer natures? by some severals
Of head-piece extraordinary? lower messes
Perchance are to this business purblind? say.

   Camillo. Business, my lord !   I think most understand
Bohemia stays here longer.

   Leontes.   Ha !

   Camillo.   Stays here longer.   220

   Leontes. Ay, but why?

   Camillo. To satisfy your highness and the entreaties
Of our most gracious mistress.

Leontes.   Satisfy!
The entreaties of your mistress! satisfy!
Let that suffice. I have trusted thee, Camillo,
With all the nearest things to my heart, as well
My chamber-counsels, wherein, priest-like, thou
Hast cleans'd my bosom, I from thee departed
Thy penitent reform'd ; but we have been
Deceiv'd in thy integrity, deceiv'd   230
In that which seems so.

Camillo.   Be it forbid, my lord!

Leontes. To bide upon 't, thou art not honest, or,
If thou inclin'st that way, thou art a coward,
Which hoxes honesty behind, restraining
From course requir'd ; or else thou must be counted
A servant grafted in my serious trust
And therein negligent ; or else a fool
That seest a game play'd home, the rich stake drawn,
And tak'st it all for jest.

Camillo.   My gracious lord,
I may be negligent, foolish, and fearful;   240
In every one of these no man is free,
But that his negligence, his folly, fear,
Among the infinite doings of the world,
Sometime puts forth. In your affairs, my lord,
If ever I were wilful-negligent,
It was my folly ; if industriously
I play'd the fool, it was my negligence,
Not weighing well the end ; if ever fearful
To do a thing, where I the issue doubted,
Whereof the execution did cry out   250
Against the non-performance, 't was a fear
Which oft infects the wisest : these, my lord,
Are such allow'd infirmities that honesty
Is never free of. But, beseech your grace,
Be plainer with me ; let me know my trespass

By it's own visage : **if I then deny it,**
'T is **none of mine.**

   Leontes.   Ha' not you seen, Camillo,—
But that **'s** past doubt ; you have, or your eye-glass
Is thicker than a cuckold's horn,—or heard,—
For to a vision so apparent rumour   260
Cannot be mute,—or thought,—for cogitation
Resides not in that man that does not think,—
My wife is slippery ?   If thou wilt confess,
Or else be impudently negative,
To have nor eyes nor ears nor thought, then say
My wife 's a hobby-horse ; say 't and justify 't.

   Camillo. I would not be a stander-by to hear
My sovereign mistress clouded so, without
My present vengeance taken.   'Shrew my heart,
You never spoke what did become you less   270
Than this ; which to reiterate were sin
As deep as that, though true.

   Leontes.   Is whispering **nothing ?**
Is leaning cheek to cheek ? is meeting noses ?
Kissing with inside lip ? stopping the career
Of laughing with a sigh ?—a note infallible
Of breaking honesty—horsing foot on foot ?
Skulking in corners ? wishing clocks more swift ?
Hours, minutes ? noon, midnight ? and all eyes
Blind with the pin and web but theirs, theirs only,
That would unseen be wicked ? is this nothing ?   280
Why, then the world and all that 's in 't is nothing :
The covering sky is nothing ; Bohemia nothing ;
My wife is nothing ; nor nothing have these nothings,
If this be nothing.

   Camillo.   Good my lord, be cur'd
Of this diseas'd opinion, and betimes ;
For 't is most dangerous.

   Leontes.   Say it be, 't is true.

Camillo. No, no, my lord.

  Leontes.   It is ; you lie, you lie :
I say thou liest, Camillo, and I hate thee,
Pronounce thee a gross lout, a mindless slave,
Or else a hovering temporizer, that   290
Canst with thine eyes at once see good and evil,
Inclining to them both. Were my wife's liver
Infected as her life, she would not live
The running of one glass.

  Camillo.   Who does infect her ?

  Leontes. Why, he that wears her like her medal, hanging
About his neck, Bohemia ;—who, if I
Had servants true about me, that bare eyes
To see alike mine honour as their profits,
Their own particular thrifts, they would do that
Which should undo more doing. Ay, and thou,   300
His cup-bearer,—whom I from meaner form
Have bench'd and rear'd to worship, who mayst see
Plainly as heaven sees earth and earth sees heaven,
How I am galled,—mightst bespice a cup,
To give mine enemy a lasting wink ;
Which draught to me were cordial.

  Camillo.   Sir, my lord,
I could do this, and that with no rash potion,
But with a lingering dram that should not work
Maliciously like poison ; but I cannot
Believe this crack to be in my dread mistress,   306
So sovereignly being honourable.
I have lov'd thee,—

  Leontes.   Make that thy question, and go rot !
Dost think I am so muddy, so unsettled,
To appoint myself in this vexation, sully
The purity and whiteness of my sheets,
Which to preserve is sleep, which being spotted
Is goads, thorns, nettles, tails of wasps,

Camillo has seen that the only way to restore order is to fall in with Leontes.

54   *THE WINTER'S TALE.*

Give scandal to the blood o' the prince my son,
Who I do think is mine and love as mine,
Without ripe moving to 't?   Would I do this?
Could man so blench?
    Camillo.   I must believe you, sir:
I do; and will fetch off Bohemia for 't:
Provided that, when he 's remov'd, your highness
Will take again your queen as yours at first,
Even for your son's sake; and thereby for sealing
The injury of tongues in courts and kingdoms
Known and allied to yours.
    Leontes.   Thou dost advise me
Even so as I mine own course have set down;
I 'll give no blemish to her honour, none.
    Camillo.   My lord,   330
Go then; and with a countenance as clear
As friendship wears at feasts, keep with Bohemia
And with your queen.   I am his cup-bearer;
If from me he have wholesome beverage,
Account me not your servant.
    Leontes.   This is all:
Do 't and thou hast the one half of my heart;
Do 't not, thou split'st thine own.
    Camillo.   I 'll do 't, my lord.
    Leontes. I will seem friendly, as thou hast advis'd me.
                                                                [Exit.

    Camillo. O miserable lady!—But, for me,
What case stand I in?   I must be the poisoner   340
Of good Polixenes; and my ground to do 't
Is the obedience to a master, one
Who in rebellion with himself will have
All that are his so too.   To do this deed,
Promotion follows.   If I could find example
Of thousands that had struck anointed kings
And flourish'd after, I 'd not do 't; but since

Nor brass nor stone nor parchment bears not one,
<u>Let villany itself forswear</u> 't.   I must
Forsake the court; <u>to do 't, or no, is certain</u>
To me <u>a break-neck.</u>—Happy star reign now !
Here comes Bohemia.

Re-enter POLIXENES.

   Polixenes.   This is strange ! methinks
My favour here begins to warp.   Not speak?—
Good day, Camillo.
   Camillo.   Hail, most royal sir !
   Polixenes. What is the news i' the court?
   Camillo.   None rare, my lord.
   Polixenes. The king hath on him such a countenance
As he had lost some province, and a region
Lov'd as he loves himself: even now I met him
With customary compliment; when he,
Wafting his eyes to the contrary and falling
A lip of much contempt, speeds from me and
So leaves me to consider what is breeding
That changeth thus his manners.
   Camillo. I dare not know, my lord.
   Polixenes. How ! dare not ! —do not?   Do you know, and
      dare not
Be intelligent to me? 't is thereabouts;
For, to yourself, what you do know you must,
And cannot say you dare not.   Good Camillo,
Your chang'd complexions are to me a mirror
Which shows me mine chang'd too; for I must be
A party in this alteration, finding
Myself thus alter'd with 't.
   Camillo.   There is a sickness
Which puts some of us in distemper, but
I cannot name the disease , and it is caught
Of you that yet are well.

Polixenes.   How! caught of me!
Make me not sighted like the basilisk;
I have look'd on thousands, who have sped the better
By my regard, but kill'd none so. Camillo,—
As you are certainly a gentleman, thereto
Clerk-like experienc'd, which no less adorns   380
Our gentry than our parents' noble names,
In whose success we are gentle,—I beseech you,
If you know aught which does behove my knowledge
Thereof to be inform'd, imprison 't not
In ignorant concealment.
     Camillo.   I may not answer.
     Polixenes. A sickness caught of me, and yet I well!
I must be answer'd. Dost thou hear, Camillo,
I conjure thee, by all the parts of man
Which honour does acknowledge,— whereof the least
Is not this suit of mine,—that thou declare   390
What incidency thou dost guess of harm
Is creeping toward me; how far off, how near;
Which way to be prevented, if to be;
If not, how best to bear it.
     Camillo.   Sir, I will tell you;
Since I am charg'd in honour and by him
That I think honourable; therefore mark my counsel,
Which must be even as swiftly follow'd as
I mean to utter it, or both yourself and me
Cry lost, and so good night!
     Polixenes.   On, good Camillo.
     Camillo. I am appointed him to murther you.   400
     Polixenes. By whom, Camillo?
     Camillo.   By the king.
     Polixenes.   For what?
     Camillo. He thinks,—nay, with all confidence he swears,
As he had seen 't or been an instrument
To vice you to 't,—that you have touch'd his queen
Forbiddenly.

Polixenes.   O, then my best blood **turn**
To an infected jelly, and my name
Be yok'd with <u>his</u> that did betray the Best!   *Judas*
Turn then my freshest reputation to
A savour that may strike the dullest nostril
Where I arrive, and my approach be shunn'd,   410
Nay, hated too, worse than the great'st infection
That e'er was heard or read!

    Camillo.   <u>Swear his thought over</u>
By each particular star in heaven and   *There is no use for you to*
By all their influences, you may as well   *swear his that over.*
Forbid the sea for to obey the moon   *(no use in swearing L.*
As or by oath remove or counsel shake   *to try to take his oath)*
The fabric of his folly, whose foundation
Is pil'd upon his faith and will continue
The standing of his body.

    Polixenes.   How should this grow?

    Camillo. <u>I know not; but I am sure 't is safer to</u>   *Shakespeare*   420
<u>Avoid what 's grown than question how 't is born.</u>   *uses the question*
If therefore you dare trust my honesty,   *to allay also the*
That lies enclosed in this trunk which you   *audience. Fact not*
Shall bear along impawn'd, away to-night!   *seems to be considered*
Your followers I will whisper to the business,
And will by twos and threes at several posterns
Clear them o' the city. For myself, I 'll put
My fortunes to your service, which are here
By this discovery lost. Be not uncertain:
For, by the honour of my parents, I   430
Have utter'd truth: which if you seek to **prove,**
I dare not stand by; nor shall you be safer
Than one condemn'd by the king's own mouth, thereon
His execution sworn.

    Polixenes.   I do believe thee;
I saw his heart in 's face. Give me thy hand
Be pilot to me, and thy places shall

Still neighbour mine.   My ships are ready, and
My people did expect my hence departure
Two days ago.   This jealousy
Is for a precious creature; as she's rare,   440
Must it be great, and as his person's mighty,
Must it be violent, and as he does conceive
He is dishonour'd by a man which ever
Profess'd to him, why, his revenges must
In that be made more bitter.   Fear o'ershades me;
Good expedition be my friend, and comfort
The gracious queen, part of his theme, but nothing
Of his ill-ta'en suspicion!—Come, Camillo;
I will respect thee as a father, if
Thou bear'st my life off hence: let us avoid.   450
   Camillo. It is in mine authority to command
The keys of all the posterns; please your highness
To take the urgent hour.   Come, sir, away.   *[Exeunt*

A CASTLE IN BOHEMIA.

OLD CORONATION CHAMBER, ROYAL PALACE, PRAGUE.

Presents picture of happy
normal homelife of queen.

Stop gap passage
while Cam + Poly
get away.

ACT II.

SCENE I. *A Room in the Palace of Leontes.*

Enter HERMIONE, MAMILLIUS, *and* Ladies.

Hermione. Take the boy to you; he so troubles me,
'T is past enduring.

    1 *Lady.*   Come, my gracious lord,
Shall I be your playfellow?

    Mamillius.   No, I'll none of you.

    1 *Lady.* Why, my sweet lord?

    Mamillius. You'll kiss me hard, and speak to me as if
I were a baby still.—I love you better.

    2 *Lady.* And why so, my lord?

    Mamillius.   Not for because
Your brows are blacker; yet black brows, they say,

Become some women best, so that there be not
Too much hair there, but in a semicircle,　　　　　10
Or a half-moon made with a pen.

   2 Lady.　　　　　　　　Who taught you this?

   Mamillius. I learnt it out of women's faces.—Pray now,
What colour are your eyebrows?

   1 Lady.　　　　　　　　Blue, my lord.

   Mamillius. Nay, that's a mock; I have seen a lady's nose
That has been blue, but not her eyebrows.

   1 Lady.　　　　　　　　Hark ye;
The queen your mother rounds apace: we shall
Present our services to a fine new prince
One of these days; and then you'd wanton with us,
If we would have you.

   2 Lady.　　　　She is spread of late
Into a goodly bulk; good time encounter her!　　　　20

   Hermione. What wisdom stirs amongst you?—Come, sir,
now
I am for you again; pray you, sit by us,
And tell's a tale.

   Mamillius.　　　　Merry or sad shall't be?

   Hermione. As merry as you will.

   Mamillius. A sad tale's best for winter; I have one
Of sprites and goblins.

   Hermione.　　　　Let's have that, good sir.
Come on, sit down: come on, and do your best
To fright me with your sprites; you're powerful at it.

   Mamillius. There was a man—

   Hermione.　　　　　　Nay, come, sit down; then on.

   Mamillius. Dwelt by a churchyard:—I will tell it softly;
Yond crickets shall not hear it.

   Hermione.　　　　　　Come on, then,　　　　31
And give't me in mine ear.

Enter LEONTES, *with* ANTIGONUS, Lords, *and* others.

Leontes. Was he met there? his train? Camillo with him?

1 *Lord.* Behind the tuft of pines I met them; never
Saw I men scour so on their way : I eyed them
Even to their ships.

Leontes.   How blest am I
In my just censure, in my true opinion!
Alack, for lesser knowledge! how accurs'd
In being so blest! There may be in the cup
A spider steep'd, and one may drink, depart,   40
And yet partake no venom, for his knowledge
Is not infected; but if one present
The abhorr'd ingredient to his eye, make known
How he hath drunk, he cracks his gorge, his sides,
With violent hefts. I have drunk, and seen the spider.
Camillo was his help in this, his pander.
There is a plot against my life, my crown;
All 's true that is mistrusted : that false villain
Whom I employ'd was pre-employ'd by him.
He has discover'd my design, and I   50
Remain a pinch'd thing; yea, a very trick
For them to play at will.—How came the posterns
So easily open?

1 *Lord.*   By his great authority,
Which often hath no less prevail'd than so
On your command.

Leontes.   I know 't too well.
Give me the boy; I am glad you did not nurse him :
Though he does bear some signs of me, yet you
Have too much blood in him.

Hermione.   What is this? sport?
Leontes. Bear the boy hence; he shall not come about her;
Away with him!—You, my lords,   60
Look on her, mark her well; be but about

To say 'she is a goodly lady,' and
The justice of your hearts will thereto add
''T is pity she 's not honest, honourable.'
Praise her but for this her without-door form,
Which on my faith deserves high speech, and straight
The shrug, the hum or ha, these petty brands
That calumny doth use—O, I am out—
That mercy does, for calumny will sear
Virtue itself; these shrugs, these hums and ha's,
When you have said 'she 's goodly,' come between   70
Ere you can say 'she 's honest:' but be 't known,
From him that has most cause to grieve it should be,
She 's an adulteress.

    Hermione.   Should a villain say so,
The most replenish'd villain in the world,
He were as much more villain; you, my lord,
Do but mistake.

    Leontes.   You have mistook, my lady,
Polixenes for Leontes.   O thou thing!
Which I 'll not call a creature of thy place,
Lest barbarism, making me the precedent,   80
Should a like language use to all degrees,
And mannerly distinguishment leave out
Betwixt the prince and beggar.—I have said
She 's an adulteress; I have said with whom:
More, she 's a traitor, and Camillo is
A federary with her, and one that knows
What she should shame to know herself
But with her most vile principal, that she 's
A bed-swerver, even as bad as those
That vulgars give bold'st titles; ay, and privy   90
To this their late escape.

    Hermione.   No, by my life,
Privy to none of this.   How will this grieve you,
When you shall come to clearer knowledge, that

You thus have publish'd me! Gentle my lord,
You scarce can right me throughly then to say
You did mistake.

    Leontes.   No; if I mistake
In those foundations which I build upon,
The centre is not big enough to bear
A school-boy's top.—Away with her! to prison!
He who shall speak for her is afar off guilty   160
But that he speaks.

    Hermione.   There's some ill planet reigns; — *fatalist*
I must be patient till the heavens look
With an aspect more favourable.—Good my lords,
I am not prone to weeping, as our sex
Commonly are.; the want of which vain dew
Perchance shall dry your pities: but I have
That honourable grief lodg'd here which burns
Worse than tears drown. Beseech you all, my lords,
With thoughts so qualified as your charities
Shall best instruct you, measure me;—and so   110
The king's will be perform'd!

    Leontes. (*To guards*) Shall I be heard?

    Hermione. Who is 't that goes with me?—Beseech your
        highness,
My women may be with me; for you see
My plight requires it.—Do not weep, good fools;
There is no cause: when you shall know your mistress
Has deserv'd prison, then abound in tears
As I come out. This action I now go on   *nobleness + resignation*
Is for my better grace.—Adieu, my lord: *I must be resigned so that*
I never wish'd to see you sorry; now   *I may grow in grace*
I trust I shall.—My women, come; you have leave.   120

    Leontes. Go, do our bidding; hence!

                    [*Exit Queen, guarded; with Ladies.*

    1 *Lord.* Beseech your highness, call the queen again.

    Antigonus. Be certain what you do, sir, lest your justice

Prove violence; in the which three great ones suffer,
Yourself, your queen, your son.

  1 *Lord*.   For her, my lord,
I dare my life lay down, and will do 't, sir,
Please you to accept it, that the queen is spotless
I' the eyes of heaven and to you,—I mean.
In this which you accuse her.

    Antigonus.   If it prove
She 's otherwise, I 'll keep my stables where   130
I lodge my wife; I 'll go in couples with her:
Than when I feel and see her no farther trust her.
For every inch of woman in the world,
Ay, every dram of woman's flesh, is false,
If she be.

    Leontes.   Hold your peaces.

  1 *Lord*.   Good my lord,—

    Antigonus. It is for you we speak, not for ourselves:
You are abus'd, and by some putter-on
That will be damn'd for 't; would I knew the villain,
I would land-damn him.

    Leontes.   Cease; no more.
You smell this business with a sense as cold   140
As is a dead man's nose; but I do see 't and feel 't,
As you feel doing thus, and see withal
The instruments that feel.

    Antigonus.   If it be so,
We need no grave to bury honesty;
There 's not a grain of it the face to sweeten
Of the whole dungy earth.

    Leontes.   What! lack I credit?

  1 *Lord*. I had rather you did lack than I, my lord,
Upon this ground; and more it would content me
To have her honour true than your suspicion,
Be blam'd for 't how you might.

    Leontes.   Why, what need we   150

Commune with you of this, but rather follow
Our forceful instigation?   Our prerogative
Calls not your counsels, but our natural goodness
Imparts this; which if you, or stupefied
Or seeming so in skill, cannot or will not
Relish a truth like us, inform yourselves
We need no more of your advice : the matter,
The loss, the gain, the ordering on 't, is all
Properly ours.

   Antigonus.   And I wish, my liege,
You had only in your silent judgment tried it,   100
Without more overture.

   Leontes.   How could that be?
Either thou art most ignorant by age,
Or thou wert born a fool.   Camillo's flight,
Added to their familiarity,—
Which was as gross as ever touch'd conjecture,
That lack'd sight only, nought for approbation
But only seeing, all other circumstances
Made up to the deed,—doth push on this proceeding.
Yet, for a greater confirmation,—
For in an act of this importance 't were   170
Most piteous to be wild,—I have dispatch'd in post
To sacred Delphos, to Apollo's temple,
Cleomenes and Dion, whom you know
Of stuff'd sufficiency.   Now from the oracle
They will bring all; whose spiritual counsel had,
Shall stop or spur me.   Have I done well?

   1 *Lord.* Well done, my lord.

   Leontes. Though I am satisfied and need no more
Than what I know, yet shall the oracle
Give rest to the minds of others, such as he *(may point to Antigonus)*   180
Whose ignorant credulity will not
Come up to the truth.   So have we thought it good
From our free person she should be confin'd,

Lest that the treachery of the two fled hence
Be left her to perform.   Come, follow us;
We are to speak in public; for this business
Will raise us all.

    Antigonus. [*Aside*] To laughter, as I take it,
If the good truth were known.   [*Exeunt.*

[handwritten annotation: Paulina like sharp tongued – vigorous, shrewish / Emilia ... tender heart / loyal / loyal]

SCENE II.   *A Prison.*

Enter PAULINA, *a* Gentleman, *and* Attendants.

    Paulina. The keeper of the prison, call to him;
Let him have knowledge who I am. — [*Exit Gentleman.*]
        Good lady,
No court in Europe is too good for thee;
What dost thou then in prison?—

        Re-enter Gentleman, *with the* Gaoler.

                Now, good sir,
You know me, do you not?
    Gaoler.   For a worthy lady,
And one whom much I honour.
    Paulina.   Pray you then,
Conduct me to the queen.
    Gaoler.   I may not, madam;
To the contrary I have express commandment.
    Paulina. Here's ado,
To lock up honesty and honour from   10
The access of gentle visitors!—Is't lawful, pray you,
To see her women? any of them? Emilia?
    Gaoler. So please you, madam,
To put apart these your attendants, I
Shall bring Emilia forth.
    Paulina.   I pray now, call her.—
Withdraw yourselves.   [*Exeunt Gentleman and Attendants.*
    Gaoler.   And, madam,
I must be present at your conference.

Paulina. Well, be 't so, prithee.—   [*Exit Gaoler.*
Here 's such ado to make no stain a stain
As passes colouring.— *uses alot of puss latin over*
something which doesn't exist.

Re-enter Gaoler, *with* EMILIA.

                         Dear gentlewoman,   20
How fares our gracious lady?
    Emilia. As well as one so great and so forlorn
May hold together; on her frights and griefs,
Which never tender lady hath borne greater,
She is something before her time deliver'd.
    Paulina. A boy?
    Emilia.   A daughter, and a goodly babe,
Lusty and like to live: the queen receives
Much comfort in 't; says 'My poor prisoner,
I am innocent as you.'
    Paulina.   I dare be sworn.— *slimy damm*
These dangerous unsafe lunes i' the king, beshrew them! 30
He must be told on 't, and he shall: the office
Becomes a woman best; I 'll take 't upon me.
If I prove honey-mouth'd, let my tongue blister
And never to my red-look'd anger be
The trumpet any more.—Pray you, Emilia,
Commend my best obedience to the queen;
If she dares trust me with her little babe,
I 'll show 't the king, and undertake to be
Her advocate to the loud'st.   We do not know
How he may soften at the sight o' the child;   40
The silence often of pure innocence
Persuades when speaking fails.
    Emilia.   Most worthy madam,
Your honour and your goodness is so evident
That your free undertaking cannot miss
A thriving issue; there is no lady living
So meet for this great errand.   Please your ladyship

To visit the next room, I 'll presently
Acquaint the queen of your most noble offer;
Who but to-day hammer'd of this design,
But durst not tempt a minister of honour,   55
Lest she should be denied.

  Paulina.   Tell her, Emilia,
I 'll use that tongue I have; if wit flow from 't
As boldness from my bosom, let 't not be doubted
I shall do good.

  Emilia.   Now be you blest for it!
I 'll to the queen; please you, come something nearer.

  Gaoler. Madam, if 't please the queen to send the babe,
I know not what I shall incur to pass it,
Having no warrant.

  Paulina.   You need not fear it, sir;
This child was prisoner to the womb, and is
By law and process of great nature thence   60
Freed and enfranchis'd, not a party to
The anger of the king, nor guilty of,
If any be, the trespass of the queen.

  Gaoler. I do believe it.

  Paulina. Do not you fear; upon mine honour, I
Will stand betwixt you and danger.   [*Exeunt.*

   SCENE III. *A Room in the Palace of Leontes.*

  Enter LEONTES, ANTIGONUS, Lords, *and* Servants.

  Leontes. Nor night nor day no rest; it is but weakness
To bear the matter thus, mere weakness. If
The cause were not in being,—part o' the cause,
She the adulteress; for the harlot king
Is quite beyond mine arm, out of the blank
And level of my brain, plot-proof; but she
I can hook to me:—say that she were gone,
Given to the fire, a moiety of my rest
Might come to me again.—Who 's there?

1 *Servant.*   **My** lord?

Leontes. How does the boy?

1 *Servant.*   He took good rest to-night;
'T is hop'd his sickness is discharg'd.   II

Leontes. To see his nobleness!
Conceiving the dishonour of his mother,
He straight declin'd, droop'd, took it deeply,
Fasten'd and fix'd the shame on 't in himself,
Threw off his spirit, his appetite, his sleep,
And downright languish'd.—Leave me solely; go,
See how he fares.—[*Exit Servant.*]   Fie, fie! no thought of
     him;
The very thought of my revenges that way
Recoil upon me: in himself too mighty,   20
And in his parties, his alliance.   Let him be
Until a time may serve; for present vengeance,
Take it on her.   Camillo and Polixenes
Laugh at me, make their pastime at my sorrow;
They should not laugh if I could reach them, nor
Shall she within my power.

Enter PAULINA, *with a child.*

1 *Lord.*   You must not enter.

Paulina. Nay, rather, good my lords, be second to me;
Fear you his tyrannous passion more, alas,
Than the queen's life? a gracious innocent soul,
More free than he is jealous.

Antigonus.   That's enough.   30

2 *Servant.* Madam, he hath not slept to-night; com-
     manded
None should come at him.

Paulina.   Not so hot, good sir;
I come to bring him sleep.   'T is such as you,
That creep like shadows by him and do sigh
At each his needless heavings, such as you

Nourish the cause of his awaking; I
Do come with words as medicinal as true,
Honest as either, to purge him of that humour
That presses him from sleep.

    Leontes.   What noise there, ho?

    Paulina. No noise, my lord; but needful conference   40
About some gossips for your highness. *gossip at baptism*

    Leontes.   How!—
Away with that audacious lady!   Antigonus,
I charg'd thee that she should not come about me;
I knew she would.

    Antigonus.   I told her so, my lord,
On your displeasure's peril and on mine,
She should not visit you.

    Leontes.   What, canst not rule her?

    Paulina. From all dishonesty he can; in this,
Unless he take the course that you have done,
Commit me for committing honour, trust it,
He shall not rule me.

    Antigonus.   La you now, you hear!   50
When she will take the rein I let her run;
But she 'll not stumble.

    Paulina.   Good my liege, I come,—
And, I beseech you, hear me, who professes
Myself your loyal servant, your physician,
Your most obedient counsellor, yet that dares
Less appear so in comforting your evils
Than such as most seem yours,—I say, I come
From your good queen.

    Leontes.   Good queen!

    Paulina.   Good queen, my lord,
Good queen, I say good queen;
And would by combat make her good, so were I   60
A man, the worst about you.

    Leontes.   Force her hence.

Paulina. Let him that makes but trifles of his eyes
First hand me; on mine own accord I 'll off,
But first I 'll do my errand.—The good queen,
For she is good, hath brought you forth a daughter,—
Here 't is,—commends it to your blessing.

> [*Laying down the child.*

Leontes. Out!
A mankind witch! Hence with her, out o' door!
A most intelligencing bawd!

Paulina. Not so:
I am as ignorant in that as you
In so entitling me, and no less honest
Than you are mad; which is enough, I 'll warrant,
As this world goes, to pass for honest.

Leontes. Traitors!
Will you not push her out? Give her the bastard.—
Thou dotard! thou art woman-tir'd, unroosted
By thy dame Partlet here. Take up the bastard;
Take 't up, I say; give 't to thy crone.

Paulina. For ever
Unvenerable be thy hands, if thou
Takest up the princess by that forced baseness
Which he has put upon 't!

Leontes. He dreads his wife.

Paulina. So I would you did; then 't were past all doubt
You 'd call your children yours.

Leontes. A nest of traitors!

Antigonus. I am none, by this good light.

Paulina. Nor I, nor any
But one that 's here, and that 's himself, for he
The sacred honour of himself, his queen's,
His hopeful son's, his babe's, betrays to slander,
Whose sting is sharper than the sword's; and will not—
For, as the case now stands, it is a curse
He cannot be compell'd to 't—once remove

The root of his opinion, which is rotten
As ever oak or stone was sound.

 Leontes.   A callat ~~Lowest of low women~~ 90
Of boundless tongue, who late hath beat her husband
And now baits me !—This brat is none of mine ;
It is the issue of Polixenes :
Hence with it, and together with the dam
Commit them to the fire !

 Paulina.   It is yours ;
And, might we lay the old proverb to your charge,
So like you, 't is the worse.—Behold, my lords,
Although the print be little, the whole matter
And copy of the father, eye, nose, lip,
The trick of 's frown, his forehead, nay, the valley, 100
The pretty dimples of his chin and cheek,
His smiles,
The very mould and frame of hand, nail, finger ;—
And thou, good goddess Nature, which hast made it
So like to him that got it, if thou hast
The ordering of the mind too, 'mongst all colours
No yellow in 't, lest she suspect, as he does, ~~it's a wise child that knows its own child~~
Her children not her husband's !

 Leontes.   A gross hag !—
And, lozel, thou art worthy to be hang'd,
That wilt not stay her tongue.

 Antigonus.   Hang all the husbands 110
That cannot do that feat, you 'll leave yourself
Hardly one subject.

 Leontes.   Once more, take her hence.

 Paulina. A most unworthy and unnatural lord
Can do no more.

 Leontes.   I 'll ha' thee burnt.

 Paulina.   I care not ;
It is an heretic that makes the fire,
Not she which burns in 't. I 'll not call you tyrant ;

But this most cruel usage of your queen,
Not able to produce more accusation
Than your own weak-hing'd fancy, something savours
Of tyranny, and will ignoble make you,   120
Yea, scandalous to the world.
  Leontes.   On your allegiance,
Out of the chamber with her! Were I a tyrant,
Where were her life? she durst not call me so,
If she did know me one. Away with her!
  Paulina. I pray you, do not push me; I 'll be gone.—
Look to your babe, my lord; 't is yours: Jove send her
A better guiding spirit!—What needs these hands?—
You, that are thus so tender o'er his follies,
Will never do him good, not one of you.—
So, so.—Farewell; we are gone.   [*Exit.*
  Leontes. Thou, traitor, hast set on thy wife to this.— 131
My child? away with 't!—Even thou, that hast
A heart so tender o'er it, take it hence
And see it instantly consum'd with fire;
Even thou and none but thou. Take it up straight;
Within this hour bring me word 't is done,
And by good testimony, or I 'll seize thy life,
With what thou else call'st thine. If thou refuse
And wilt encounter with my wrath, say so;
The bastard brains with these my proper hands   140
Shall I dash out. Go, take it to the fire;
For thou set'st on thy wife.
  Antigonus.   I did not, sir;
These lords, my noble fellows, if they please,
Can clear me in 't.
  Lords.   We can; my royal liege,
He is not guilty of her coming hither.
  Leontes. You 're liars all.
  1 *Lord.* Beseech your highness, give us better credit:
We have always truly serv'd you, and beseech you

So to esteem of us; and on our knees we beg,
As recompense of our dear services   150
Past and to come, that you do change this purpose,
Which being so horrible, so bloody, must
Lead on to some foul issue : we all kneel.
    Leontes. I am a feather for each wind that blows.—
Shall I live on to see this bastard kneel
And call me father? better burn it now
Than curse it then.   But be it; let it live.—
It shall not neither.—You, sir, come you hither ;
You that have been so tenderly officious   *here used as*
With **Lady** Margery, your <u>midwife</u> there, "*old women*" 160
To save this bastard's life,—for 't is a bastard,
So sure as this beard 's grey,—what will you adventure
To save this brat's life?
    Antigonus.   Any thing, my lord,
That my ability may undergo
And nobleness impose; at least thus much:
I 'll pawn the little blood which I have left
To save the innocent;—any thing possible.
    Leontes. It shall be possible.   Swear by this sword
Thou wilt perform my bidding.
    Antigonus.   I will, my lord.
    Leontes. Mark and perform it, see'st thou; for the fail   170
Of any point in 't shall not only be
Death to thyself, but to thy lewd-tongu'd wife,
Whom for this time we pardon.   We enjoin thee,
As thou art liege-man to us, that thou carry
This female bastard hence, and that thou bear it
To some remote and desert place quite out
Of our dominions, and that there thou leave it,
Without more mercy, to it own protection
And favour of the climate.   As by strange fortune
It came to us, I do in justice charge thee,   180
On thy soul's peril and thy body's torture,

That thou commend it strangely to some place
Where chance may nurse or end it.   Take it up.

   Antigonus. I swear to do this, though a present death
Had been more merciful.—Come on, poor babe;
Some powerful spirit instruct the kites and ravens
To be thy nurses! Wolves and bears, they say,
Casting their savageness aside, have done
Like offices of pity.—Sir, be prosperous
In more than this deed does require! And blessing   191
Against this cruelty fight on thy side,
Poor thing, condemn'd to loss!   [*Exit with the child.*

   Leontes.   No, I'll not rear
Another's issue.

               Enter a Servant.

   Servant.   Please your highness, posts
From those you sent to the oracle are come
An hour since; Cleomenes and Dion,
Being well arriv'd from Delphos, are both landed,
Hasting to the court.

   1 *Lord.*   So please you, sir, their speed
Hath been beyond account.

   Leontes.   Twenty-three days
They have been absent: 't is good speed; foretells
The great Apollo suddenly will have   200
The truth of this appear. Prepare you, lords;
Summon a session, that we may arraign
Our most disloyal lady, for, as she hath
Been publicly accus'd, so shall she have
A just and open trial. While she lives
My heart will be a burthen to me. Leave me,
And think upon my bidding.   [*Exeunt.*

A SEAPORT IN SICILY.

ACT III.

Scene I. *A Seaport in Sicilia.*

Enter Cleomenes *and* Dion.

Cleomenes. The climate 's delicate, the air most sweet,
Fertile the isle, the temple much surpassing
The common praise it bears.

    Dion. I shall report,
For most it caught me, the celestial habits,—
Methinks I so should term them,—and the reverence
Of the grave wearers. O, the sacrifice!

How ceremonious, solemn, and unearthly
It was i' the offering!

Cleomenes.   But of all, the burst
And the ear-deafening voice o' the oracle,
Kin to Jove's thunder, so surpris'd my sense,   10
That I was nothing.

Dion.   If the event o' the journey
Prove as successful to the queen—O, be 't so!—
As it hath been to us rare, pleasant, speedy,
The time is worth the use on 't.

Cleomenes.   Great Apollo
Turn all to the best! These proclamations,
So forcing faults upon Hermione,
I little like.

Dion.   The violent carriage of it
Will clear or end the business; when the oracle,
Thus by Apollo's great divine seal'd up,
Shall the contents discover, something rare   20
Even then will rush to knowledge.—Go: fresh horses!—
And gracious be the issue!   [*Exeunt.*

Scene II.   *A Court of Justice.*

Enter Leontes, Lords, *and* Officers.

Leontes. This sessions, to our great grief we pronounce,
Even pushes 'gainst our heart; the party tried
The daughter of a king, our wife, and one
Of us too much belov'd.—Let us be clear'd
Of being tyrannous, since we so openly
Proceed in justice, which shall have due course,
Even to the guilt or the purgation.
Produce the prisoner.

Officer. It is his highness' pleasure that the queen
Appear in person here in court.—Silence!   10

Enter HERMIONE *guarded;* PAULINA *and* Ladies *attending.*

Leontes. Read the indictment.

Officer. [Reads] '*Hermione, queen to the worthy Leontes,*
king of Sicilia, thou art here accused and arraigned of high
treason, in committing adultery with Polixenes, king of Bohe-
mia, and conspiring with Camillo to take away the life of
our sovereign lord the king, thy royal husband; the pretence
whereof being by circumstances partly laid open, thou, Her-
mione, contrary to the faith and allegiance of a true subject,
didst counsel and aid them, for their better safety, to fly away
by night.'   20

Hermione. Since what I am to say must be but that
Which contradicts my accusation, and
The testimony on my part no other
But what comes from myself, it shall scarce boot me
To say 'not guilty;' mine integrity,
Being counted falsehood, shall, as I express it,
Be so receiv'd. But thus: if powers divine
Behold our human actions, as they do,
I doubt not then but innocence shall make
False accusation blush and tyranny   30
Tremble at patience.—You, my lord, best know,
Who least will seem to do so, my past life
Hath been as continent, as chaste, as true,
As I am now unhappy; which is more
Than history can pattern, though devis'd
And play'd to take spectators. For behold me,
A fellow of the royal bed, which owe
A moiety of the throne, a great king's daughter,
The mother to a hopeful prince, here standing,
To prate and talk for life and honour fore   40
Who please to come and hear. For life, I prize it
As I weigh grief, which I would spare; for honour,
'T is a derivative from me to mine,

And only that I stand for.   I appeal
To your own conscience, sir, before Polixenes
Came to your court, how I was in your grace,
How merited to be so; since he came,
With what encounter so uncurrent I
Have strain'd to appear thus : if one jot beyond
The bound of honour, or in act or will
That way inclining, harden'd be the hearts
Of all that hear me, and my near'st of kin
Cry fie upon my grave !

Leontes.   I ne'er heard yet
That any of these bolder vices wanted
Less impudence to gainsay what they did
Than to perform it first.

Hermione.   That 's true enough;
Though 't is a saying, sir, not due to me.

Leontes. You will not own it.

Hermione.   More than mistress of
Which comes to me in name of fault, I must not
At all acknowledge.   For Polixenes,
With whom I am accus'd, I do confess
I lov'd him as in honour he requir'd,
With such a kind of love as might become
A lady like me, with a love even such,
So and no other, as yourself commanded;
Which not to have done I think had been in me
Both disobedience and ingratitude
To you and toward your friend, whose love had spoke,
Even since it could speak, from an infant, freely
That it was yours.   Now, for conspiracy,
I know not how it tastes; though it be dish'd
For me to try how : all I know of it
Is that Camillo was an honest man ;
And why he left your court, the gods themselves,
Wotting no more than I, are ignorant.

Leontes. You knew of his departure, as you know
What you have underta'en to do in 's absence.

Hermione. Sir,
You speak a language that I understand not;
My life stands in the level of your dreams, 86
Which I 'll lay down.

Leontes.   Your actions are my dreams;
You had a bastard by Polixenes,
And I but dream'd it. As you were past all shame,—
Those of your fact are so—so past all truth:
Which to deny concerns more than avails; for as
Thy brat hath been cast out, like to itself,
No father owning it,—which is, indeed,
More criminal in thee than it,—so thou
Shalt feel our justice, in whose easiest passage
Look for no less than death.

Hermione.   Sir, spare your threats: 90
The bug which you would fright me with I seek.
To me can life be no commodity:
The crown and comfort of my life, your favour,
I do give lost; for I do feel it gone,
But know not how it went. My second joy
And first-fruits of my body, from his presence
I am barr'd, like one infectious. My third comfort
Starr'd most unluckily, is from my breast,
The innocent milk in it most innocent mouth,
Hal'd out to murther; myself on every post 100
Proclaim'd a strumpet; with immodest hatred
The child-bed privilege denied, which longs
To women of all fashion; lastly, hurried
Here to this place, i' the open air, before
I have got strength of limit. Now, my liege,
Tell me what blessings I have here alive,
That I should fear to die? Therefore proceed.
But yet hear this; mistake me not: for life,

I prize it not a straw; but for mine honour,
Which I would free, if I shall be condemn'd   110
Upon surmises, all proofs sleeping else
But what your jealousies awake, I tell you
'T is rigour and not law.—Your honours all,
I do refer me to the oracle;
Apollo be my judge!

   1 *Lord.*   This your request
Is altogether just; therefore bring forth,
And in Apollo's name, his oracle.   [*Exeunt certain Officers.*

   Hermione. The Emperor of Russia was my father;
O that he were alive, and here beholding
His daughter's trial! that he did but see   120
The flatness of my misery,—yet with eyes
Of pity, not revenge!

          Re-enter Officers, *with* CLEOMENES *and* DION.

   Officer. You here shall swear upon this sword of justice,
That you, Cleomenes and Dion, have
Been both at Delphos, and from thence have brought
This seal'd-up oracle, by the hand deliver'd
Of great Apollo's priest, and that since then
You have not dar'd to break the holy seal
Nor read the secrets in 't.

   Cleomenes, Dion.   All this we swear.

   Leontes. Break up the seals and read.   130

   Officer. [Reads] '*Hermione is chaste; Polixenes blameless;
Camillo a true subject; Leontes a jealous tyrant; his innocent babe truly begotten; and the king shall live without an
heir, if that which is lost be not found.*'

   Lords. Now blessed be the great Apollo!

   Hermione.   Praised!

   Leontes. Hast thou read truth?

   Officer.   Ay, my lord; even so
As it is here set down.

Leontes. There is no truth at all i' the oracle :
The sessions shall proceed ; this is mere falsehood.

Enter Servant.

Servant. My lord the king, the king!

Leontes.   What is the business?

Servant. O sir, I shall be hated to report it !   141
The prince your son, with mere conceit and fear
Of the queen's speed, is gone.

Leontes.   How ! gone !

Servant.   Is dead.

Leontes. Apollo 's angry ; and the heavens themselves
Do strike at my injustice.—[*Hermione swoons.*] How now
      there !

Paulina. This news is mortal to the queen ; look down
And see what death is doing.

Leontes.   Take her hence :
Her heart is but o'ercharg'd ; she will recover.—
I have too much believ'd mine own suspicion.—
Beseech you, tenderly apply to her   150
Some remedies for life.—

      [*Exeunt Paulina and Ladies, with Hermione.*
                        Apollo, pardon
My great profaneness 'gainst thine oracle !
I 'll reconcile me to Polixenes,
New woo my queen, recall the good Camillo,
Whom I proclaim a man of truth, of mercy ;
For, being transported by my jealousies
To bloody thoughts and to revenge, I chose
Camillo for the minister to poison
My friend Polixenes ; which had been done,
But that the good mind of Camillo tardied   160
My swift command, though I with death and with
Reward did threaten and encourage him,
Not doing 't and being done. He, most humane

And fill'd with honour, to my kingly guest
Unclasp'd my practice, quit his fortunes here,
Which you knew great, and to the hazard
Of all incertainties himself commended,
No richer than his honour.—How he glisters
Thorough my rust! and how his piety
Does my deeds make the blacker!

Re-enter PAULINA.

Paulina.   Woe the while!   17❬
O, cut my lace, lest my heart, cracking it,
Break too.
    1 *Lord.*   What fit is this, good lady?
    Paulina. What studied torments, tyrant, hast for me?
What wheels? racks? fires? what flaying? boiling
In leads or oils? what old or newer torture
Must I receive, whose every word deserves
To taste of thy most worst?   Thy tyranny
Together working with thy jealousies,
Fancies too weak for boys, too green and idle
For girls of nine,—O, think what they have done,   180
And then run mad indeed, stark mad! for all
Thy bygone fooleries were but spices of it.
That thou betray'dst Polixenes, 't was nothing;
That did but show thee, of a fool, inconstant
And damnable ingrateful: nor was 't much,
Thou wouldst have poison'd good Camillo's honour,
To have him kill a king; poor trespasses,
More monstrous standing by: whereof I reckon
The casting forth to crows thy baby-daughter
To be or none or little; though a devil   190
Would have shed water out of fire ere done 't:
Nor is 't directly laid to thee, the death
Of the young prince, whose honourable thoughts,
Thoughts high for one so tender, cleft the heart

That could conceive a gross and foolish sire
Blemish'd his gracious dam: this is not, no,
Laid to thy answer: but the last,—O lords,
When I have said, cry woe!—the queen, the queen,
The sweet'st, dear'st creature 's dead, and vengeance for 't
Not dropp'd down yet.

    1 *Lord.*   The higher powers forbid!   200

    Paulina. I say she 's dead; I 'll swear 't. If word nor
        oath
Prevail not, go and see; if you can bring
Tincture or lustre in her lip, her eye,
Heat outwardly or breath within, I 'll serve you
As I would do the gods.—But, O thou tyrant!
Do not repent these things, for they are heavier
Than all my woes can stir; therefore betake thee
To nothing but despair.   A thousand knees
Ten thousand years together, naked, fasting,
Upon a barren mountain, and still winter   210
In storm perpetual, could not move the gods
To look that way thou wert.

    Leontes.   Go on, go on!
Thou canst not speak too much; I have deserv'd
All tongues to talk their bitterest.

    1 *Lord.*   Say no more;
Howe'er the business goes, you have made fault
I' the boldness of your speech.

    Paulina.   I am sorry for 't;
All faults I make, when I shall come to know them,
I do repent.   Alas! I have show'd too much
The rashness of a woman; he is touch'd
To the noble heart.—What 's gone and what 's past help
Should be past grief: do not receive affliction   220
At my petition; I beseech you, rather
Let me be punish'd, that have minded you
Of what you should forget.   Now, good my liege,

Sir, royal sir, forgive a foolish woman;
The love I bore your queen—lo, fool again!—
I 'll speak of her no more, nor of your children;
I 'll not remember you of my own lord,
Who is lost too : take your patience to you,
And I 'll say nothing.

    Leontes.   Thou didst speak but well   230
When most the truth ; which I receive much better
Than to be pitied of thee.   Prithee, bring me
To the dead bodies of my queen and son :
One grave shall be for both ; upon them shall
The causes of their death appear, unto
Our shame perpetual.   Once a day I 'll visit
The chapel where they lie, and tears shed there
Shall be my recreation ; so long as nature
Will bear up with this exercise, so long
I daily vow to use it.   Come and lead me   240
Unto these sorrows.   *[Exeunt.*

SCENE III.   *Bohemia.*   *A Desert Country near the Sea.*

    Enter ANTIGONUS *with a Child, and a* Mariner.

Antigonus. Thou art perfect then, our ship hath touch'd upon
The deserts of Bohemia?

    Mariner.   Ay, my lord, and fear
We have landed in ill time ; the skies look grimly
And threaten present blusters.   In my conscience,
The heavens with that we have in hand are angry
And frown upon 's.

    Antigonus. Their sacred wills be done !—Go, get aboard ;
Look to thy bark : I 'll not be long before
I call upon thee.

    Mariner. Make your best haste, and go not   10
Too far i' the land : 't is like to be loud weather ;

Dream of Antigonus must be dramatic justificaten for his death.

Besides, this place is famous for the creatures
Of prey that keep upon 't.
    Antigonus.   Go thou away ;
I 'll follow instantly.
    Mariner.   I am glad at heart
To be so rid o' the business.   [*Exit.*
    Antigonus.   Come, poor babe :
i have heard, but not believ'd, the spirits o' the dead
May walk again ; if such thing be, thy mother
Appear'd to me last night, for ne'er was dream
So like a waking.   To me comes a creature,
Sometimes her head on one side, some another ;   20
I never saw a vessel of like sorrow,
So fill'd and so becoming : in pure white robes,
Like very sanctity, she did approach
My cabin where I lay ; thrice bow'd before me,
And gasping to begin some speech, her eyes
Became two spouts. The fury spent, anon
Did this break from her : 'Good Antigonus,
Since fate, against thy better disposition,
Hath made thy person for the thrower-out
Of my poor babe, according to thine oath,   30
Places remote enough are in Bohemia,
There weep and leave it crying ; and, for the babe
Is counted lost for ever, Perdita,
I prithee, call 't. For this ungentle business,
Put on thee by my lord, thou ne'er shalt see
Thy wife Paulina more.' And so, with shrieks,
She melted into air. Affrighted much,
I did in time collect myself and thought
This was so and no slumber. Dreams are toys ;
Yet for this once, yea, superstitiously,   40
I will be squar'd by this.   I do believe
Hermione hath suffer'd death, and that
Apollo would, this being indeed the issue

Of King Polixenes, it should here be laid,
Either for life or death, upon the earth
Of its right father. —Blossom, speed thee well!
There lie, and there thy character : there these ;   *money +*
Which may, if fortune please, both breed thee, pretty,   *identification*
And still rest thine.—The storm begins.—Poor wretch,
That for thy mother's fault art thus expos'd   50
To loss and what may follow!—Weep I cannot,
But my heart bleeds ; and most accurs'd am I
To be by oath enjoin'd to this.—Farewell!
The day frowns more and more ; thou 'rt like to have
A lullaby too rough : I never saw
The heavens so dim by day.   A savage clamour!—
Well may I get aboard!—This is the chase ;
I am gone for ever.   [*Exit, pursued by a bear.*

Enter a Shepherd.

Shepherd. I would there were no age between sixteen
and three-and-twenty, or that youth would sleep out the
intervening rest ; for there is nothing in the between but wronging the
ancientry, stealing, fighting—Hark you now! Would any
but these boiled brains of nineteen and two-and-twenty   *dumb bells*
hunt this weather? They have scared away two of my   *a boiled*
best sheep, which I fear the wolf will sooner find than the *brain is*
master ; if any where I have them, 't is by the seaside, *of no use.*
browsing of ivy. Good luck, an 't be thy will! what have
we here? Mercy on 's, a barne ; a very pretty barne! A
boy or a child, I wonder? A pretty one ; a very pretty
spade one. Sure, some scape ; though I am not bookish, yet I
can read waiting-gentlewoman in the scape. I 'll take it
up for pity : yet I 'll tarry till my son come ; he hallooed
but even now. Whoa, ho, hoa!   73

Enter Clown. (*not who feels—rather*
a country bumpkin.)

Clown. Hilloa, loa!

Shepherd. What, art so near? If thou 'lt see a thing to talk on when thou art dead and rotten, come hither. What ailest thou, man?

Clown. I have seen two such sights, by sea and by land! but I am not to say it is a sea, for it is now the sky; betwixt the firmament and it you cannot thrust a bodkin's point.

Shepherd. Why, boy, how is it?   81

Clown. I would you did but see how it chafes, how it rages, how it takes up the shore! but that 's not to the point. O, the most piteous cry of the poor souls! sometimes to see 'em, and not to see 'em; now the ship boring the moon with her main-mast, and anon swallowed with yest and froth, as you 'd thrust a cork into a hogshead. And then for the land-service, to see how the bear tore out his shoulder-bone; how he cried to me for help and said his name was Antigonus, a nobleman. But to make an end of the ship, to see how the sea flap-dragoned it: but, first, how the poor souls roared, and the sea mocked them; and how the poor gentleman roared and the bear mocked him, both roaring louder than the sea or weather.   94

Shepherd. Name of mercy, when was this, boy?

Clown. Now, now; I have not winked since I saw these sights: the men are not yet cold under water, nor the bear half dined on the gentleman; he 's at it now.

Shepherd. Would I had been by, to have helped the old man!   100

Clown. I would you had been by the ship side, to have helped her, there your charity would have lacked footing.

Shepherd. Heavy matters! heavy matters! but look thee here, boy. Now bless thyself; thou mettest with things dying, I with things new-born. Here 's a sight for thee; look thee, a bearing-cloth for a squire's child! look thee here; take up, take up, boy; open 't. So, let 's see; it was told me I should be rich by the fairies. This is some changeling; open 't. What 's within, boy?

Clown. You 're a made old man; if the sins of your youth are forgiven you, you 're well to live.   Gold! all gold!   111

Shepherd. This is fairy gold, boy, and 't will prove so; up with 't, keep it close: home, home, the next way.   We are lucky, boy; and to be so still requires nothing but secrecy.   Let my sheep go; come, good boy, the next way home.

Clown. Go you the next way with your findings.   I 'll go see if the bear be gone from the gentleman and how much he hath eaten; they are never curst but when they are hungry: if there be any of him left, I 'll bury it.

Shepherd. That 's a good deed.   If thou mayest discern by that which is left of him what he is, fetch me to the sight of him.   122

Clown. Marry, will I; and you shall help to put him i' the ground.

Shepherd. 'T is a lucky day, boy, and we 'll do good deeds on 't.   [*Exeunt*

The running of one glass (i. 2. 294).

[Margin annotations:] will be ever plentiful · do it not spoil or it disappear · The better the day the better the deed. used to rationalize or justify an act done when we feel it should not be. · means The better the day, the better your deed should be.

ACT IV.

Scene I.

Enter Time, *the* Chorus.

Time. **I** that please some, try all, both joy and **terror**
Of good and bad, that makes and unfolds error,
Now take upon me, in the name of Time,

To use my wings.   Impute it not a crime
To me or my swift passage, that I slide
O'er sixteen years and leave the growth untried
Of that wide gap, since it is in my power
To o'erthrow law and in one self-born hour
To plant and o'erwhelm custom.   Let me pass
The same I am, ere ancient'st order was
Or what is now receiv'd: I witness to
The times that brought them in; so shall I do
To the freshest things now reigning, and make stale
The glistering of this present, as my tale
Now seems to it.   Your patience this allowing,
I turn my glass and give my scene such growing
As you had slept between.   Leontes leaving,
The effects of his fond jealousies so grieving
That he shuts up himself, imagine me,
Gentle spectators, that I now may be
In fair Bohemia; and remember well,
I mention'd a son o' the king's, which **Florizel**
I now name to you; and with speed so pace
To speak of Perdita, now grown in grace
Equal with wondering.   What of her ensues
I list not prophesy; but let Time's news
Be known when 't is brought forth.   A shepherd's **daughter**,
And what to her adheres, which follows after,
Is the argument of Time.   Of this allow,
If ever you have spent time worse ere now;
If never, yet that Time himself doth say
He wishes earnestly you never **may**.

[*Exit.*

*virtually the author coming out + speaking
It is informationally unnecessary
Dramatically constitutive*

SCENE II.   *Bohemia.   The Palace of Polixenes.*
Enter POLIXENES *and* CAMILLO.

Polixenes. I pray thee, good Camillo, be no more import-
unate : 't is a sickness denying thee any thing ; a death to
grant this.

Camillo. It is fifteen years since I saw my country ; though
I have for the most part been aired abroad, I desire to lay my
bones there.   Besides, the penitent king, my master, hath sent
for me ; to whose feeling sorrows I might be some allay, or I
o'erween to think so, which is another spur to my departure.

Polixenes. As thou lovest me, Camillo, wipe not out the
rest of thy services by leaving me now.   The need I have of
thee thine own goodness hath made ; better not to have had
thee than thus to want thee.   Thou, having made me busi-
nesses which none without thee can sufficiently manage, must
either stay to execute them thyself or take away with thee the
very services thou hast done ; which if I have not enough considered, as too much I cannot, to be more thankful to thee
shall be my study, and my profit therein the heaping friendships.   Of that fatal country, Sicilia, prithee speak no more ;
whose very naming punishes me with the remembrance of
that penitent, as thou callest him, and reconciled king, my
brother; whose loss of his most precious queen and children
are even now to be afresh lamented.   Say to me, when saw-
est thou the Prince Florizel, my son ?   Kings are no less unhappy, their issue not being gracious, than they are in losing
them when they have approved their virtues.   25

Camillo. Sir, it is three days since I saw the prince.   What
his happier affairs may be, are to me unknown; but I have
missingly noted, he is of late much retired from court and is
less frequent to his princely exercises than formerly he hath
appeared.

Polixenes. I have considered so much, Camillo, and with

some care; so far that I have eyes under my service which look upon his removedness, from whom I have this intelligence, that he is seldom from the house of a most homely shepherd; a man, they say, that from very nothing, and beyond the imagination of his neighbours, is grown into an unspeakable estate.

Camillo. I have heard, sir, of such a man, who hath a daughter of most rare note; the report of her is extended more than can be thought to begin from such a cottage. 40

Polixenes. That's likewise part of my intelligence, but, I fear, the angle that plucks our son thither. Thou shalt accompany us to the place; where we will, not appearing what we are, have some question with the shepherd; from whose simplicity I think it not uneasy to get the cause of my son's resort thither. Prithee, be my present partner in this business, and lay aside the thoughts of Sicilia.

Camillo. I willingly obey your command.

Polixenes. My best Camillo! We must disguise ourselves.

[*Exeunt.*

SCENE III. *A Road near the Shepherd's Cottage.*

Enter AUTOLYCUS, *singing.*

When daffodils begin to peer,
  With heigh! the doxy over the dale,
Why, then comes in the sweet o' the year:
  For the red blood reigns in the winter's pale.

The white sheet bleaching on the hedge,
  With heigh! the sweet birds, O, how they sing!
Doth set my pugging tooth on edge;
  For a quart of ale is a dish for a king.

The lark, that tirra-lirra chants,
  With heigh! with heigh! the thrush and the jay, 10
Are summer songs for me and my aunts,
  While we lie tumbling in the hay.

I have served Prince Florizel and in my time wore three-
pile, but now I am out of service;

> *But shall I go mourn for that, my dear?*
> *The pale moon shines by night;*
> *And when I wander here and there,*
>   *I then do most go right.*

> *If tinkers may have leave to live,*
>   *And bear the sow-skin budget,*   20
> *Then my account I well may give,*
>   *And in the stocks avouch it.*

My traffic is sheets; when the kite builds, look to lesser linen.
My father named me Autolycus; who being, as I am, littered
under Mercury, was likewise a snapper-up of unconsidered
trifles. With die and drab I purchased this caparison, and
my revenue is the silly cheat. Gallows and knock are too
powerful on the highway; beating and hanging are terrors to
me: for the life to come, I sleep out the thought of it. — A
prize! a prize!   30

Enter Clown.

Clown. Let me see: every 'leven wether tods; every tod
yields pound and odd shilling; fifteen hundred shorn,—
what comes the wool to?

Autolycus. [*Aside*] If the springe hold, the cock 's mine.

Clown. I cannot do 't without counters. Let me see; what
am I to buy for our sheep-shearing feast? Three pound of
sugar, five pound of currants, rice,—what will this sister of
mine do with rice? But my father hath made her mistress
of the feast, and she lays it on. She hath made me four-and-
twenty nosegays for the shearers, three-man songmen all,
and very good ones; but they are most of them means and
bases; but one puritan amongst them, and he sings psalms
to hornpipes. I must have saffron to colour the warden
pies; mace; dates?—none, that 's out of my note; nutmegs,

seven ; a race or two of ginger, but that I may beg ; four pound of prunes, and as many of raisins o' the sun.

Autolycus. O that ever I was born !

[*Grovelling on the ground.*

Clown. I' the name of me—

Autolycus. O, help me, help me ! pluck but off these rags ; and then, death, death !   50

Clown. Alack, poor soul ! thou hast need of more rags to lay on thee, rather than have these off.

Autolycus. O sir, the loathsomeness of them offends me more than the stripes I have received, which are mighty ones and millions.

Clown. Alas, poor man ! a million of beating may come to a great matter.

Autolycus. I am robbed, sir, and beaten ; my money and apparel ta'en from me, and these detestable things put upon me.   60

Clown. What, by a horseman, or a footman ?

Autolycus. A footman, sweet sir, a footman.

Clown. Indeed, he should be a footman by the garments he has left with thee ; if this be a horseman's coat, it hath seen very hot service. Lend me thy hand, I 'll help thee ; come, lend me thy hand.

Autolycus. O, good sir, tenderly, O !

Clown. Alas, poor soul !

Autolycus. O, good sir, softly, good sir ! I fear, sir, my shoulder-blade is out.   70

Clown. How now ! canst stand ?

Autolycus. [*Picking his pocket*] Softly, dear sir ; good sir, softly. You ha' done me a charitable office.

Clown. Dost lack any money ? I have a little money for thee.

Autolycus. No, good, sweet sir ; no, I beseech you, sir. I have a kinsman not past three quarters of a mile hence, unto whom I was going ; I shall there have money, or any thing

I want. Offer me no money, I pray you; that kills my
heart.   80

Clown. What manner of fellow was he that robbed you?

Autolycus. A fellow, sir, that I have known to go about
with troll-my-dames. I knew him once a servant of the
prince; I cannot tell, good sir, for which of his virtues it was,
but he was certainly whipped out of the court.

Clown. His vices, you would say; there 's no virtue
whipped out of the court: they cherish it to make it stay
there; and yet it will no more but abide.   88

Autolycus. Vices, I would say, sir. I know this man well:
he hath been since an ape-bearer; then a process-server, a
bailiff; then he compassed a motion of the Prodigal Son,
and married a tinker's wife within a mile where my land and
living lies; and, having flown over many knavish professions,
he settled only in rogue: some call him Autolycus.

Clown. Out upon him! prig, for my life, prig; he haunts
wakes, fairs, and bear-baitings.

Autolycus. Very true, sir; he, sir, he; that 's the rogue that
put me into this apparel.

Clown. Not a more cowardly rogue in all Bohemia; if
you had but looked big and spit at him, he 'd have run.   100

Autolycus. I must confess to you, sir, I am no fighter: I
am false of heart that way; and that he knew, I warrant him.

Clown. How do you now?

Autolycus. Sweet sir, much better than I was; I can stand
and walk. I will even take my leave of you, and pace softly towards my kinsman's.

Clown. Shall I bring thee on the way?

Autolycus. No, good-faced sir; no, sweet sir.

Clown. Then fare thee well; I must go buy spices for our
sheep-shearing.   110

Autolycus. Prosper you, sweet sir!—[*Exit Clown.*] Your
purse is not hot enough to purchase your spice. I 'll be
with you at your sheep-shearing too; if I make not this

cheat bring out another and the shearers prove sheep, let
me be unroll'd and my name put in the book of virtue!

[*Sings*] *Jog on, jog on, the foot-path way,*
   And merrily hent the stile-a ;
   A merry heart goes all the day,
   Your sad tires in a mile-a.   [*Exit.*

SCENE IV. *The Shepherd's Cottage.*
Enter FLORIZEL *and* PERDITA.

Florizel. These your unusual weeds to each part of you
Do give a life ; no shepherdess, but Flora
Peering in April's front. This your sheep-shearing
Is as a meeting of the petty gods,
And you the queen on 't.
 Perdita.   Sir, my gracious lord,
To chide at your extremes it not becomes me ;
O, pardon, that I name them ! Your high self,
The gracious mark o' the land, you have obscur'd
With a swain's wearing, and me, poor lowly maid,
Most goddess-like prank'd up. But that our feasts 10
In every mess have folly and the feeders
Digest it with a custom, I should blush
To see you so attir'd, sworn, I think,
To show myself a glass.
 Florizel.   I bless the time
When my good falcon made her flight across
Thy father's ground.
 Perdita.   Now Jove afford you cause !
To me the difference forges dread ; your greatness
Hath not been us'd to fear. Even now I tremble
To think your father, by some accident,
Should pass this way as you did. O, the Fates ! 20
How would he look, to see his work so noble
Vilely bound up ? What would he say ? Or how

Should I, in these my borrow'd flaunts, behold
The sternness of his presence?
  Florizel.   Apprehend
Nothing but jollity. The gods themselves,
Humbling their deities to love, have taken
The shapes of beasts upon them: Jupiter
Became a bull, and bellow'd; the green Neptune
A ram, and bleated; and the fire-rob'd god,
Golden Apollo, a poor humble swain,   30
As I seem now. Their transformations
Were never for a piece of beauty rarer,
Nor in a way so chaste,—since my desires
Run not before mine honour, nor my lusts
Burn hotter than my faith.
  Perdita.   O, but, sir,
Your resolution cannot hold, when 't is
Oppos'd, as it must be, by the power of the king;
One of these two must be necessities,
Which then will speak,—that you must change this purpose,
Or I my life.
  Florizel.   Thou dearest Perdita,   40
With these forc'd thoughts, I prithee, darken not
The mirth o' the feast. Or I 'll be thine, my fair,
Or not my father's. For I cannot be
Mine own, nor any thing to any, if
I be not thine. To this I am most constant,
Though destiny say no. Be merry, gentle;
Strangle such thoughts as these with any thing
That you behold the while. Your guests are coming;
Lift up your countenance, as it were the day
Of celebration of that nuptial which   50
We two have sworn shall come.
  Perdita.   O lady Fortune,
Stand you auspicious!
  Florizel.   See, your guests approach;

Address yourself to entertain them sprightly,
And let 's be red with mirth.

Enter Shepherd, Clown, Mopsa, Dorcas, *and others, with*
Polixenes *and* Camillo *disguised.*

  Shepherd. Fie, daughter! when my old wife liv'd, upon
This day she was both pantler, butler, cook,
Both dame and servant; welcom'd all, serv'd all;
Would sing her song and dance her turn; now here,
At upper end o' the table, now i' the middle;
On his shoulder, and his; her face o' fire   60
With labour; and the thing she took to quench it,
She would to each one sip.   You are retir'd,
As if you were a feasted one, and not
The hostess of the meeting.   Pray you, bid
These unknown friends to 's welcome; for it is
A way to make us better friends, more known.
Come, quench your blushes and present yourself
That which you are, mistress o' the feast; come on,
And bid us welcome to your sheep-shearing,
As your good flock shall prosper.
  Perdita.   [*To Polixenes*] Sir, welcome!   70
It is my father's will I should take on me
The hostess-ship o' the day.—[*To Camillo*] You 're welcome,
      sir.—
Give me those flowers there, Dorcas.—Reverend sirs,
For you there 's rosemary and rue; these keep
Seeming and savour all the winter long:
Grace and remembrance be to you both,
And welcome to our shearing!
  Polixenes.   Shepherdess,—
A fair one are you—well you fit our ages
With flowers of winter.
  Perdita.   Sir, the year growing ancient,—
Not yet on summer's death, nor on the birth   80

Of trembling winter,—the fairest flowers o' the season
Are our carnations and streak'd gillyvors,
Which some call nature's bastards : of that kind
Our rustic garden 's barren ; and I care not
To get slips of them.

    Polixenes.   Wherefore, gentle maiden,
Do you neglect them?

    Perdita.   For I have heard it said
There is an art which in their piedness shares
With great creating nature.

    Polixenes.   Say there be ;
Yet nature is made better by no mean
But nature makes that mean : so, over that art
Which you say adds to nature, is an art
That nature makes.   You see, sweet maid, we marry
A gentler scion to the wildest stock,
And make conceive a bark of baser kind
By bud of nobler race.   This is an art
Which does mend nature,—change it rather ; but
The art itself is nature.

    Perdita.   So it is.

    Polixenes. Then make your garden rich in gillyvors,
And do not call them bastards.

    Perdita.   I 'll not put
The dibble in earth to set one slip of them ;
No more than were I painted I would wish
This youth should say 't were well and only therefore
Desire to breed by me.—Here 's flowers for you :
Hot lavender, mints, savory, marjoram ;
The marigold, that goes to bed wi' the sun
And with him rises weeping : these are flowers
Of middle summer, and I think they are given
To men of middle age.   You 're very welcome.

    Camillo. I should leave grazing, were I of your flock,
And only live by gazing.

Perdita.   Out, alas!   110
You'd be so lean, that blasts of January
Would blow you through and through. — Now, my fair'st
    friend,
I would I had some flowers o' the spring that **might**
Become your time of day; and yours, and yours,
That wear upon your virgin branches yet
Your maidenheads growing.   O Proserpina,
For the flowers **now that** frighted thou let'st **fall**
From Dis's waggon! daffodils,
That come before the swallow dares, and take   *charm*
The winds of March with beauty; violets dim,   120
But sweeter than the lids of Juno's eyes
Or Cytherea's breath; pale primroses,
That die unmarried, ere they can behold
Bright Phœbus in his strength—a malady
Most incident to maids; bold oxlips and
The crown imperial; lilies of all kinds,
The flower-de-luce being one!   O, these I lack,
To make you garlands of, and my sweet friend,
To strew him o'er and o'er!
    Florizel.   What, like a corse?
    Perdita. No, like a bank for love to lie and play on,   130
Not like a corse; or if,—not to be buried,
But quick and in mine arms.   Come, take your flowers:
Methinks I play as I have seen them do
In Whitsun pastorals; sure this robe of mine
Does change my disposition.
    Florizel.   What you do
Still betters what is done.   When you speak, sweet,
I'd have you do it ever; when you sing,
I'd have you buy and sell so, so give alms,
Pray so; and, for the ordering your affairs,
To sing them too: when you do dance, I wish you   140
A wave o' the sea, that you might ever do

Nothing but that; move still, still so,
And own no other function.   Each your **doing**,
So singular in each particular,
Crowns what you are doing in the present deed,
That all your acts are queens.

    Perdita.   O Doricles,
Your praises are too large; but that your youth,
And the true blood which peeps so fairly through 't,
Do plainly give you out an unstain'd shepherd,
With wisdom I might fear, my Doricles,   150
You woo'd me the false way.

    Florizel.   I think you **have**
As little skill to fear as I have purpose
To put you to 't.—But come; our dance, I **pray** :
Your hand, my Perdita; so turtles pair,
That never mean to part.

    Perdita.   I 'll swear for 'em.

    Polixenes. This is the prettiest low-born lass that ever
Ran on the green-sward; nothing she does or seems
But smacks of something greater than herself,
Too noble for this place.

    Camillo.   He tells her something
That makes her blood look out; good sooth, she is   160
The queen of curds and cream.

    Clown.   Come on, strike up !

    Dorcas. Mopsa must be your mistress; marry, garlic,
To mend her kissing with !

    Mopsa.   Now, in good time !

    Clown. Not a word, a word; we stand upon our **manners.**—
Come, strike up !

    [*Music.   Here a dance of Shepherds and Shepherdesses.*

    Polixenes. Pray, good shepherd, what fair **swain** is this
Which dances with your daughter?

    Shepherd. They call him Doricles; and boasts himself
To have a worthy feeding: but I have it

Upon his own report and I believe it;   170
He looks like sooth.   He says he loves my daughter:
I think so too; for never gaz'd the moon
Upon the water as he 'll stand and read
As 't were my daughter's eyes : and, to be plain,
I think there is not half a kiss to choose
Who loves another best.

   Polixenes.   She dances featly.

   Shepherd. So she does any thing; though I report it,
That should be silent.   If young Doricles
Do light upon her, she shall bring him that
Which he not dreams of.   180

Enter Servant.

   Servant. O master, if you did but hear the pedler at the
door, you would never dance again after a tabor and pipe;
no, the bagpipe could not move you.   He sings several tunes
faster than you 'll tell money; he utters them as he had eat-
en ballads and all men's ears grew to his tunes.

   Clown. He could never come better; he shall come in.   I
love a ballad but even too well, if it be doleful matter merrily set down, or a very pleasant thing indeed and sung
lamentably.   189

   Servant. He hath songs for man or woman, of all sizes;
no milliner can so fit his customers with gloves : he has the
prettiest love-songs for maids; so without bawdry, which is
strange; with such delicate burthens of dildos and fadings,
'jump her and thump her;' and where some stretch-mouthed
rascal would, as it were, mean mischief and break a foul gap
into the matter, he makes the maid to answer 'Whoop, do
me no harm, good man;' puts him off, slights him, with
'Whoop, do me no harm, good man.'

   Polixenes. This is a brave fellow.

   Clown. Believe me, thou talkest of an admirable conceited
fellow.   Has he any unbraided wares?   201

He doesn't want skillful ware as they may not be tricky — he wants honest goods.

braided = skillfully made.

Servant. He hath ribbons of all the colours i' the rainbow; points more than all the lawyers in Bohemia can learnedly handle, though they come to him by the gross; inkles, caddisses, cambrics, lawns: why, he sings 'em over as they were gods or goddesses; you would think a smock were a she-angel, he so chants to the sleeve-hand and the work about the square on 't.

Clown. Prithee bring him in; and let him approach singing.

Perdita. Forewarn him that he use no scurrilous words in 's tunes.   [*Exit Servant.*

Clown. You have of these pedlers, that have more in them than you 'd think, sister.   212

Perdita. Ay, good brother, or go about to think.

Enter AUTOLYCUS, *singing.*

> *Lawn as white as driven snow;*
> *Cyprus black as e'er was crow;*
> *Gloves as sweet as damask roses;*
> *Masks for faces and for noses;*
> *Bugle bracelet, necklace amber,*
> *Perfume for a lady's chamber;*   220
> *Golden quoifs and stomachers,*
> *For my lads to give their dears;*
> *Pins and poking-sticks of steel,*
> *What maids lack from head to heel:*
> *Come buy of me, come; come buy, come buy;*
> *Buy, lads, or else your lasses cry: come buy.*

Clown. If I were not in love with Mopsa, thou shouldst take no money of me; but being enthralled as I am, it will also be the bondage of certain ribbons and gloves.

Mopsa. I was promised them against the feast; but they come not too late now.   231

Dorcas. He hath promised you more than that, or there be liars.

Mopsa. He hath paid you all he promised you; may be,

he has paid you more, which will shame you to give him again.

Clown. Is there no manners left among maids? Is there not milking-time, when you are going to bed, or kiln-hole, to whistle off these secrets, but you must be tittle-tattling before all our guests? 't is well they are whispering: charm your tongues, and not a word more.   241

Mopsa. I have done. Come, you promised me a tawdry-lace and a pair of sweet gloves.

Clown. Have I not told thee how I was cozened by the way and lost all my money?

Autolycus. And indeed, sir, there are cozeners abroad; therefore it behoves men to be wary.

Clown. Fear not thou, man, thou shalt lose nothing here.

Autolycus. I hope so, sir; for I have about me many parcels of charge.   250

Clown. What hast here? ballads?

Mopsa. Pray now, buy some; I love a ballad in print o' life, for then we are sure they are true.

Autolycus. Here 's one to a very doleful tune, how a usurer's wife longed to eat adders' heads and toads carbonadoed.

Mopsa. Is it true, think you?

Autolycus. Very true, and but a month old.

Dorcas. Bless me from marrying a usurer!

Mopsa. Pray you now, buy it.   260

Clown. Come on, lay it by: and let 's first see moe ballads; we 'll buy the other things anon.

Autolycus. Here 's another ballad of a fish, that appeared upon the coast on Wednesday the fourscore of April, forty thousand fathom above water, and sung this ballad against the hard hearts of maids; it was thought she was a woman and was turned into a cold fish. The ballad is very pitiful and as true.

Dorcas. Is it true too, think you?

Autolycus. Five justices' hands at it, and witnesses more than my pack will hold. 271

Clown. Lay it by too : another.

Autolycus. This is a merry ballad, but a very pretty one.

Mopsa. Let 's have some merry ones.

Autolycus. Why, this is a passing merry one and goes to the tune of 'Two maids wooing a man:' there 's scarce a maid westward but she sings it ; 't is in request, I can tell you.

Mopsa. We can both sing it : if thou 'lt bear a part, thou shalt hear ; 't is in three parts. 280

Dorcas. We had the tune on 't a month ago.

Autolycus. I can bear my part ; you must know 't is my occupation. Have at it with you.

Song.

Autolycus.	*Get you hence, for I must go*
	Where it fits not you to know.
Dorcas.	*Whither ?*
Mopsa.	*O, whither ?*
Dorcas.	*Whither ?*
Mopsa.	*It becomes thy oath full well,*
	Thou to me thy secrets tell. 290
Dorcas.	*Me too, let me go thither.*
Mopsa.	*Or thou goest to the grange or mill.*
Dorcas.	*If to either, thou dost ill.*
Autolycus.	*Neither.*
Dorcas.	*What, neither ?*
Autolycus.	*Neither.*
Dorcas.	*Thou hast sworn my love to be.*
Mopsa.	*Thou hast sworn it more to me :*
	Then whither goest ? say, whither ?

Clown. We 'll have this song out anon by ourselves ; my father and the gentlemen are in sad talk, and we 'll not trouble them. Come, bring away thy pack after me.—

Wenches, I 'll buy for you both.—Pedler, let 's have the first
choice.—Follow me, girls.　　　[*Exit with Dorcas and Mopsa.*

Autolycus. And you shall pay well for 'em.　　　　305
　　　　　　　　　　　　　　　　[*Follows singing*

> *Will you buy any tape,*
> *Or lace for your cape,*
> *My dainty duck, my dear-a?*
> *Any silk, any thread,*
> *Any toys for your head,*　　　　310
> *Of the new'st and fin'st, fin'st wear-a?*
> *Come to the pedler;*
> *Money 's a meddler,*
> *That doth utter all men's ware-a.*　　　　[*Exit.*

Re-enter Servant.

Servant. Master, there is three carters, three shepherds,
three neat-herds, three swine-herds, that have made themselves all men of hair, they call themselves Saltiers, and
they have a dance which the wenches say is a gallimaufry
of gambols, because they are not in 't; but they themselves
are o' the mind, if it be not too rough for some that know
little but bowling, it will please plentifully.　　　321

Shepherd. Away! we 'll none on 't; here has been too
much homely foolery already.—I know, sir, we weary you.

Polixenes. You weary those that refresh us. Pray, let 's
see these four threes of herdsmen.

Servant. One three of them, by their own report, sir, hath
danced before the king; and not the worst of the three but
jumps twelve foot and a half by the squire.

Shepherd. Leave your prating: since these good men are
pleased, let them come in; but quickly now.　　　330

Servant. Why, they stay at door, sir.　　　　[*Exit.*

Here a dance of twelve Satyrs.

Polixenes. O, father, you 'll know more of that hereafter.—
[*To Camillo*] Is it not too far gone?—'T is time to part them.

He 's simple and tells much.—[*To Florizel*] How now, fair
    shepherd !
Your heart is full of something that does take
Your mind from feasting.   Sooth, when I was young
And handed love as you do, I was wont
To load my she with knacks.   I would have ransack'd
The pedler's silken treasury and have pour'd it
To her acceptance ; you have let him go   340
And nothing marted with him.   If your lass
Interpretation should abuse and call this
Your lack of love or bounty, you were straited
For a reply, at least if you make a care
Of happy holding her.
    Florizel.   Old sir, I know
She prizes not such trifles as these are :
The gifts she looks from me are pack'd and lock'd
Up in my heart; which I have given already,
But not deliver'd.—O, hear me breathe my life
Before this ancient sir, who, it should seem,   350
Hath sometime lov'd ! I take thy hand, this hand,
As soft as dove's down and as white as it,
Or Ethiopian's tooth, or the fann'd snow that 's bolted
By the northern blasts twice o'er.
    Polixenes.   What follows this ?—
How prettily the young swain seems to wash
The hand was fair before !—I have put you out :
But to your protestation ; let me hear
What you profess.
    Florizel.   Do, and be witness to 't.
    Polixenes. And this my neighbour too ?
    Florizel.   And he, and more
Than he, and men, the earth, the heavens, and all :   360
That, were I crown'd the most imperial monarch,
Thereof most worthy, were I the fairest youth
That ever made eye swerve, had force and knowledge

More than was ever man's, I would not prize them
Without her love; for her employ them all,
Commend them and condemn them to her service
Or to their own perdition.

    Polixenes.   Fairly offer'd.
    Camillo. This shows a sound affection.
    Shepherd.   But, my daughter,
Say you the like to him?
    Perdita.   I cannot speak
So well, nothing so well; no, nor mean better: 370
By the pattern of mine own thoughts I cut out
The purity of his.
    Shepherd.   Take hands, a bargain!—
And, friends unknown, you shall bear witness to 't;
I give my daughter to him, and will make
Her portion equal his.
    Florizel.   O, that must be
I' the virtue of your daughter: one being dead,
I shall have more than you can dream of yet;
Enough then for your wonder. But, come on,
Contract us fore these witnesses.
    Shepherd.   Come, your hand;
And, daughter, yours.
    Polixenes.   Soft, swain, awhile, beseech you;   380
Have you a father?
    Florizel.   I have; but what of him?
    Polixenes. Knows he of this?
    Florizel.   He neither does nor shall
    Polixenes. Methinks a father
Is at the nuptial of his son a guest
That best becomes the table. Pray you once more,
Is not your father grown incapable
Of reasonable affairs? is he not stupid
With age and altering rheums? can he speak? hear?
Know man from man? dispute his own estate?

Lies he not bed-rid? and again does nothing   390
But what he did being childish?

   Florizel.   No, good sir;
He has his health and ampler strength indeed,
Than most have of his age.

   Polixenes.   By my white beard,
You offer him, if this be so, a wrong
Something unfilial.   Reason my son
Should choose himself a wife, but as good reason
The father, all whose joy is nothing else
But fair posterity, should hold some counsel
In such a business.

   Florizel.   I yield all this;
But for some other reasons, my grave sir,   400
Which 't is not fit you know, I not acquaint
My father of this business.

   Polixenes.   Let him know 't.

   Florizel. He shall not.

   Polixenes.   Prithee, let him.

   Florizel.   No, he must not.

   Shepherd. Let him, my son; he shall not need to grieve
At knowing of thy choice.

   Florizel.   Come, come, he must not.—
Mark our contract.

   Polixenes.   Mark your divorce, young sir,
                             [Discovering himself.
Whom son I dare not call; thou art too base
To be acknowledg'd, thou a sceptre's heir,
That thus affects a sheep-hook!—Thou old traitor,
I am sorry that by hanging thee I can   410
But shorten thy life one week.—And thou, fresh piece
Of excellent witchcraft, who of force must know
The royal fool thou cop'st with,—

   Shepherd.   O, my heart!

   Polixenes. I'll have thy beauty scratch'd with briers, and made

More homely than thy state.—For thee, fond boy,
If I may ever know thou dost but sigh
That thou no more shalt see this knack, as never
I mean thou shalt, we 'll bar thee from succession;
Not hold thee of our blood, no, not our kin,
Far than Deucalion off.   Mark thou my words: 420
Follow us to the court.—Thou churl, for this time,
Though full of our displeasure, yet we free thee
From the dead blow of it.—And you, enchantment,—
Worthy enough a herdsman; yea, him too,
That makes himself, but for our honour therein,
Unworthy thee,—if ever henceforth thou
These rural latches to his entrance open,
Or hoop his body more with thy embraces,
I will devise a death as cruel for thee
As thou art tender to 't.   [*Exit.*

   Perdita.   Even here undone!   430
I was not much afeard; for once or twice
I was about to speak and tell him plainly,
The selfsame sun that shines upon his court
Hides not his visage from our cottage, but
Looks on alike.—Will 't please you, sir, be gone?
I told you what would come of this.   Beseech you,
Of your own state take care; this dream of mine,—
Being now awake, I 'll queen it no inch farther,
But milk my ewes and weep.
   Camillo.   Why, how now, father?
Speak ere thou diest.
   Shepherd.   I cannot speak, nor think,   440
Nor dare to know that which I know.—O sir!
You have undone a man of fourscore three,
That thought to fill his grave in quiet, yea,
To die upon the bed my father died,
To lie close by his honest bones; but now
Some hangman must put on my shroud, and lay me

Where no priest shovels in dust.—O cursed wretch,
That knew'st this was the prince, and wouldst adventure
To mingle faith with him!—Undone! undone!
If I might die within this hour, I have liv'd   450
To die when I desire.   [*Exit.*

    Florizel.   Why look you so upon me?
I am but sorry, not afeard; delay'd,
But nothing alter'd.   What I was, I am;
More straining on for plucking back, not following
My leash unwillingly.

    Camillo.   Gracious my lord,
You know your father's temper: at this time
He will allow no speech, which I do guess
You do not purpose to him; and as hardly
Will he endure your sight as yet, I fear.
Then, till the fury of his highness settle,   460
Come not before him.

    Florizel.   I not purpose it.
I think,—Camillo?

    Camillo.   Even he, my lord.

    Perdita. How often have I told you 't would be thus!
How often said, my dignity would last
But till 't were known!

    Florizel.   It cannot fail but by
The violation of my faith; and then
Let nature crush the sides o' the earth together
And mar the seeds within!   Lift up thy looks:
From my succession wipe me, father; I
Am heir to my affection.

    Camillo.   Be advis'd.   470

    Florizel. I am, and by my fancy: if my reason
Will thereto be obedient, I have reason;
If not, my senses, better pleas'd with madness,
Do bid it welcome.

    Camillo.   This is desperate, sir.

Florizel. So call it; but it does fulfil my vow:
I needs must think it honesty.   Camillo,
Not for Bohemia, nor the pomp that may
Be thereat glean'd, for all the sun sees or
The close earth wombs or the profound sea hides
In unknown fathoms, will I break my oath   48c
To this my fair belov'd: therefore, I pray you,
As you have ever been my father's honour'd friend,
When he shall miss me,—as, in faith, I mean not
To see him any more,—cast your good counsels
Upon his passion; let myself and fortune
Tug for the time to come.   This you may know
And so deliver,—I am put to sea
With her whom here I cannot hold on shore;
And most opportune to our need I have
A vessel rides fast by, but not prepar'd   49c
For this design.   What course I mean to hold
Shall nothing benefit your knowledge, nor
Concern me the reporting.

   Camillo.   O my lord!
I would your spirit were easier for advice,
Or stronger for your need.

   Florizel.   Hark, Perdita.—[*Drawing her aside.*
I 'll hear you by and by.

   Camillo.   He 's irremovable,
Resolv'd for flight.   Now were I happy, if
His going I could frame to serve my turn,
Save him from danger, do him love and honour,
Purchase the sight again of dear Sicilia   50c
And that unhappy king, my master, whom
I so much thirst to see.

   Florizel.   Now, good Camillo;
I am so fraught with curious business that
I leave out ceremony.

   Camillo.   Sir, I think

You have heard of my poor services, i' the love
That I have borne your father?
    Florizel.   Very nobly
Have you deserv'd; it is my father's music
To speak your deeds, not little of his care
To have them recompens'd as thought on.
    Camillo.   Well, my lord,
If you may please to think I love the king   510
And through him what is nearest to him, which is
Your gracious self, embrace but my direction:
If your more ponderous and settled project
May suffer alteration, on mine honour,
I 'll point you where you shall have such receiving
As shall become your highness; where you may
Enjoy your mistress, from the whom, I see,
There 's no disjunction to be made, but by—
As heavens forefend!—your ruin; marry her,
And, with my best endeavours in your absence,   520
Your discontenting father strive to qualify
And bring him up to liking.
    Florizel.   How, Camillo,
May this, almost a miracle, be done?
That I may call thee something more than man,
And after that trust to thee.
    Camillo.   Have you thought on
A place whereto you 'll go?
    Florizel.   Not any yet;
But as the unthought-on accident is guilty
To what we wildly do, so we profess
Ourselves to be the slaves of chance and flies
Of every wind that blows.
    Camillo.   Then list to me: 530
This follows, if you will not change your purpose
But undergo this flight, make for Sicilia,
And there present yourself and your fair princess,

For so I see she must be, fore Leontes;
She shall be habited as it becomes
The partner of your bed.   Methinks I see
Leontes opening his free arms and weeping
His welcomes forth; asks thee the son forgiveness,
As 't were i' the father's person; kisses the hands
Of your fresh princess; o'er and o'er divides him   540
'Twixt his unkindness and his kindness; the one
He chides to hell, and bids the other grow
Faster than thought or time.

    Florizel.   Worthy Camillo,
What colour for my visitation shall I
Hold up before him?

    Camillo.   Sent by the king your father
To greet him and to give him comforts.   Sir,
The manner of your bearing towards him, with
What you as from your father shall deliver,
Things known betwixt us three, I 'll write you down:
The which shall point you forth at every sitting   550
What you must say; that he shall not perceive
But that you have your father's bosom there
And speak his very heart.

    Florizel.   I am bound to you;
There is some sap in this.

    Camillo.   A cause more promising
Than a wild dedication of yourselves
To unpath'd waters, undream'd shores, most certain
To miseries enough; no hope to help you,
But as you shake off one to take another;
Nothing so certain as your anchors, who
Do their best office, if they can but stay you   560
Where you 'll be loath to be.   Besides you know
Prosperity 's the very bond of love,
Whose fresh complexion and whose heart together
Affliction alters.

Perdita.   One of these is true;
I think affliction may subdue the cheek,
But not take in the mind.
     Camillo.   Yea, say you so?
There shall not at your father's house these seven years
Be born another such.
     Florizel.   My good Camillo,
She is as forward of her breeding as
She is i' the rear o' our birth.
     Camillo.   I cannot say 't is pity   570
She lacks instructions, for she seems a mistress
To most that teach.
     Perdita.   Your pardon, sir; for this
I 'll blush you thanks.
     Florizel.   My prettiest Perdita!—
But O, the thorns we stand upon!—Camillo,
Preserver of my father, now of me,
The medicine of our house, how shall we do?
We are not furnish'd like Bohemia's son,
Nor shall appear in Sicilia.
     Camillo.   My lord,
Fear none of this.   I think you know my fortunes
Do all lie there; it shall be so my care   580
To have you royally appointed as if
The scene you play were mine.   For instance, sir,
That you may know you shall not want,—one word.
                              [*They talk aside.*

                Re-enter AUTOLYCUS.

Autolycus. Ha, ha! what a fool Honesty is! and Trust, his
sworn brother, a very simple gentleman!   I have sold all
my trumpery; not a counterfeit stone, not a ribbon, glass,
pomander, brooch, table-book, ballad, knife, tape, glove, shoe-
tie, bracelet, horn-ring, to keep my pack from fasting.   They
throng who should buy first, as if my trinkets had been hallowed and brought a benediction to the buyer: by which

means I saw whose purse was best in picture; and what I saw, to my good use I remembered. My clown, who wants but something to be a reasonable man, grew so in love with the wenches' song, that he would not stir his pettitoes till he had both tune and words; which so drew the rest of the herd to me that all their other senses stuck in ears. I could have filed keys off that hung in chains; no hearing, no feeling, but my sir's song, and admiring the nothing of it. So that in this time of lethargy I picked and cut most of their festival purses; and had not the old man come in with a whoo-bub against his daughter and the king's son and scared my choughs from the chaff, I had not left a purse alive in the whole army. [*Camillo, Florizel, and Perdita come forward.*

Camillo. Nay, but my letters, by this means being there
So soon as you arrive, shall clear that doubt.   605

Florizel. And those that you'll procure from King Leontes—
Camillo. Shall satisfy your father.
Perdita.   Happy be you!
All that you speak shows fair.
Camillo.   Who have we here?—
                    [*Seeing Autolycus.*
We'll make an instrument of this, omit
Nothing may give us aid.

Autolycus. If they have overheard me now, why, hanging.

Camillo. How now, good fellow! why shakest thou so?
Fear not, man; here's no harm intended to thee.   613

Autolycus. I am a poor fellow, sir.

Camillo. Why, be so still; here's nobody will steal that from thee: yet for the outside of thy poverty we must make an exchange; therefore discase thee instantly,—thou must think there's a necessity in 't,—and change garments with this gentleman. Though the pennyworth on his side be the worst, yet hold thee, there's some boot.

Autolycus. I am a poor fellow, sir.—[*Aside*] I know ye well enough.   622

Camillo. Nay, prithee, dispatch ; the gentleman is half
flayed already.

Autolycus. Are you in earnest, sir?—[*Aside*] I smell the
trick on 't.

Florizel. Dispatch, I prithee.

Autolycus. Indeed, I have had earnest ; but I cannot with
conscience take it.

Camillo. Unbuckle, unbuckle.—   63c
        [*Florizel and Autolycus exchange garments*
Fortunate mistress,—let my prophecy
Come home to ye !—you must retire yourself
Into some covert : take your sweetheart's hat
And pluck it o'er your brows, muffle your face,
Dismantle you, and, as you can, disliken
The truth of your own seeming ; that you may—
For I do fear eyes over—to shipboard
Get undescried.

Perdita.   I see the play so lies
That I must bear a part.

Camillo.   No remedy.—
Have you done there?

Florizel.   Should I now meet my father,   640
He would not call me son.

Camillo.   Nay, you shall have no hat.—
                                [*Giving it to Perdita.*
Come, lady, come.—Farewell, my friend.

Autolycus.   Adieu, sir.

Florizel. O Perdita, what have we twain forgot !
Pray you, a word.

Camillo. [*Aside*] What I do next, shall be to tell the king
Of this escape and whither they are bound :
Wherein my hope is I shall so prevail
To force him after ; in whose company
I shall review Sicilia, for whose sight
I have a woman's longing.

Florizel.   Fortune speed us!— 650
Thus we set on, Camillo, to the sea-side.

Camillo. The swifter speed the better.

                    [*Exeunt Florizel, Perdita and Camillo.*

Autolycus. I understand the business, I hear it. To have
an open ear, a quick eye, and a nimble hand, is necessary
for a cut-purse ; a good nose is requisite also, to smell out
work for the other senses. I see this is the time that the
unjust man doth thrive. What an exchange had this been
without boot! What a boot is here with this exchange!
Sure the gods do this year connive at us, and we may do
any thing extempore. The prince himself is about a piece
of iniquity, stealing away from his father with his clog at his
heels. If I thought it were a piece of honesty to acquaint
the king withal, I would not do 't : I hold it the more
knavery to conceal it ; and therein am I constant to my
profession.— 665

                    Re-enter Clown *and* Shepherd.

Aside, aside ; here is more matter for a hot brain. Every
lane's end, every shop, church, session, hanging, yields a
careful man work.

Clown. See, see ; what a man you are now! There is no
other way but to tell the king she 's a changeling and none
of your flesh and blood. 671

Shepherd. Nay, but hear me.

Clown. Nay, but hear me.

Shepherd. Go to, then.

Clown. She being none of your flesh and blood, your
flesh and blood has not offended the king ; and so your
flesh and blood is not to be punished by him. Show those
things you found about her, those secret things, all but what
she has with her. This being done, let the law go whistle ;
I warrant you. 680

Shepherd. I will tell the king all, every word, yea, and his
son's pranks too ; who, I may say, is no honest man, neither

to his father nor to me, to go about to make me the king's
brother-in-law.

Clown. Indeed, brother-in-law was the farthest off you
could have been to him, and then your blood had been the
dearer by I know how much an ounce.

Autolycus. [*Aside*] Very wisely, puppies!

Shepherd. Well, let us to the king; there is that in this
fardel will make him scratch his beard.   690

Autolycus. [*Aside*] I know not what impediment this complaint may be to the flight of my master.

Clown. Pray heartily he be at palace.

Autolycus. [*Aside*] Though I am not naturally honest, I
am so sometimes by chance; let me pocket up my pedler's
excrement.—[*Takes off his false beard.*] How now, rustics!
whither are you bound?

Shepherd. To the palace, an it like your worship.

Autolycus. Your affairs there, what, with whom, the condition of that fardel, the place of your dwelling, your names,
your ages, of what having, breeding, and any thing that is
fitting to be known, discover.   702

Clown. We are but plain fellows, sir.

Autolycus. A lie! you are rough and hairy. Let me
have no lying; it becomes none but tradesmen, and they
often give us soldiers the lie: but we pay them for it with
stamped coin, not stabbing steel; therefore they do not
give us the lie.

Clown. Your worship had like to have given us one, if
you had not taken yourself with the manner.   710

Shepherd. Are you a courtier, an 't like you, sir?

Autolycus. Whether it like me or no, I am a courtier.
Seest thou not the air of the court in these enfoldings?
hath not my gait in it the measure of the court? receives
not thy nose court-odour from me? reflect I not on thy
baseness court-contempt? Thinkest thou, for that I insinuate, or touze from thee thy business, I am therefore no

courtier? I am courtier cap-a-pe ; and one that will either
push on or pluck back thy business there : whereupon I
command thee to open thy affair.   720

Shepherd. My business, sir, is to the king.

Autolycus. What advocate hast thou to him?

Shepherd. I know not, an 't like you.

Clown. Advocate 's the court-word for a pheasant ; say
you have none.

Shepherd. None, sir ; I have no pheasant, cock nor hen.

Autolycus. How blest are we that are not simple men !
Yet nature might have made me as these are,
Therefore I will not disdain.

Clown. This cannot be but a great courtier.   730

Shepherd. His garments are rich, but he wears them not
handsomely.

Clown. He seems to be the more noble in being fantasti-
cal : a great man, I 'll warrant; I know by the picking on 's
teeth.

Autolycus. The fardel there? what 's i' the fardel? Where-
fore that box?

Shepherd. Sir, there lies such secrets in this fardel and
box, which none must know but the king ; and which he
shall know within this hour, if I may come to the speech of
him.   741

Autolycus. Age, thou hast lost thy labour.

Shepherd. Why, sir?

Autolycus. The king is not at the palace ; he is gone
aboard a new ship to purge melancholy and air himself :
for, if thou beest capable of things serious, thou must know
the king is full of grief.

Shepherd. So 't is said, sir ; about his son, that should
have married a shepherd's daughter.

Autolycus. If that shepherd be not in hand-fast, let him
fly ; the curses he shall have, the tortures he shall feel, will
break the back of man, the heart of monster.   752

Clown. Think you so, sir?

Autolycus. Not he alone shall suffer what wit can make heavy and vengeance bitter, but those that are germane to him, though removed fifty times, shall all come under the hangman; which though it be great pity, yet it is necessary. An old sheep-whistling rogue, a ram-tender, to offer to have his daughter come into grace! Some say he shall be stoned; but that death is too soft for him, say I. Draw our throne into a sheep-cote! all deaths are too few, the sharpest too easy.   762

Clown. Has the old man e'er a son, sir, do you hear, an 't like you, sir?

Autolycus. He has a son, who shall be flayed alive; then 'nointed over with honey, set on the head of a wasp's nest; then stand till he be three quarters and a dram dead; then recovered again with aqua-vitæ or some other hot infusion; then, raw as he is, and in the hottest day prognostication proclaims, shall he be set against a brick-wall, the sun looking with a southward eye upon him, where he is to behold him with flies blown to death. But what talk we of these traitorly rascals, whose miseries are to be smiled at, their offences being so capital? Tell me, for you seem to be honest plain men, what you have to the king: being something gently considered, I 'll bring you where he is aboard, tender your persons to his presence, whisper him in your behalfs; and if it be in man besides the king to effect your suits, here is man shall do it.   779

Clown. He seems to be of great authority: close with him, give him gold; and though authority be a stubborn bear, yet he is oft led by the nose with gold. Show the inside of your purse to the outside of his hand, and no more ado. Remember, stoned and flayed alive!

Shepherd. An 't please you, sir, to undertake the business for us, here is that gold I have; I 'll make it as much more, and leave this young man in pawn till I bring it you.

Autolycus. After I have done what I promised?

Shepherd. Ay, sir.

Autolycus. Well, give me the moiety.—Are you a party in this business?
　　　　　　　　　　　　　　　　　　　　791

Clown. In some sort, sir ; but though my case be a pitiful one, I hope I shall not be flayed out of it.

Autolycus. O, that 's the case of the shepherd's son ; hang him, he 'll be made an example.

Clown. Comfort, good comfort! We must to the king and show our strange sights : he must know 't is none of your daughter nor my sister ; we are gone else.—Sir, I will give you as much as this old man does when the business is performed, and remain, as he says, your pawn till it be brought you.
　　　　　　　　　　　　　　　　　　　　801

Autolycus. I will trust you. Walk before toward the sea-side ; go on the right hand : I will but look upon the hedge and follow you.

Clown. We are blest in this man, as I may say, even blest.

Shepherd. Let 's before, as he bids us ; he was provided to do us good.　　　　　　　[*Exeunt Shepherd and Clown.*

Autolycus. If I had a mind to be honest, I see Fortune would not suffer me ; she drops booties in my mouth. I am courted now with a double occasion, gold and a means to do the prince my master good ; which who knows how that may turn back to my advancement? I will bring these two moles, these blind ones, aboard him : if he think it fit to shore them again, and that the complaint they have to the king concerns him nothing, let him call me rogue for being so far officious ; for I am proof against that title and what shame else belongs to 't. To him will I present them ; there may be matter in it.　　　　　　　[*Exit.*

O, she 's warm! (v. 3. 109).

ACT V.

SCENE I.   *A Room in the Palace of Leontes.*

Enter LEONTES, CLEOMENES, DION, PAULINA, *and* Servants.

Cleomenes. Sir, you have done enough, and have per-
form'd
A saint-like sorrow.   No fault could you make,
Which you have not redeem'd; indeed, paid down

Lords interrupted by in succession
they were all her.

More penitence than done trespass.   At the last,
Do as the heavens have done, forget your evil ;
With them forgive yourself.

   Leontes.   Whilst I remember
Her and her virtues, I cannot forget
My blemishes in them, and so still think of
The wrong I did myself ; which was so much
That heirless it hath made my kingdom, and   10
Destroy'd the sweet'st companion that e'er man
Bred his hopes out of.

   Paulina.   True, too true, my lord ;
If, one by one, you wedded all the world,
Or from the all that are took something good,
To make a perfect woman, she you kill'd
Would be unparallel'd.

   Leontes.   I think so.   Kill'd !
She I kill'd !   I did so : but thou strikest me
Sorely, to say I did ; it is as bitter
Upon thy tongue as in my thought.   Now, good now,
Say so but seldom.

   Cleomenes.   Not at all, good lady ;   20
You might have spoken a thousand things tnat would
Have done the time more benefit and grac'd
Your kindness better.

   Paulina.   You are one of those
Would have him wed again.

   Dion.   If you would not so,
You pity not the state, nor the remembrance
Of his most sovereign name : consider little
What dangers, by his highness' fail of issue,
May drop upon his kingdom and devour
Incertain lookers-on.   What were more holy
Than to rejoice the former queen is well ?   30
What holier than, for royalty's repair,
For present comfort and for future good.

To bless the bed of majesty again
With a sweet fellow to 't?

    Paulina.   There is none worthy,
Respecting her that 's gone.   Besides, the gods
Will have fulfill'd their secret purposes;
For has not the divine Apollo said,
Is 't not the tenour of his oracle,
That King Leontes shall not have an heir
Till his lost child be found? which that it shall,   40
Is all as monstrous to our human reason
As my Antigonus to break his grave
And come again to me; who, on my life,
Did perish with the infant.   'T is your counsel
My lord should to the heavens be contrary,
Oppose against their wills.—[*To Leontes*] Care not for
    issue;
The crown will find an heir.   Great Alexander
Left his to the worthiest; so his successor
Was like to be the best.

    Leontes.   Good Paulina,—
Who hast the memory of Hermione,   50
I know, in honour,—O that ever I
Had squar'd me to thy counsel! then, even now,
I might have look'd upon my queen's full eyes,
Have taken treasure from her lips—

    Paulina.   And left them
More rich for what they yielded.

    Leontes.   Thou speak'st truth.
No more such wives; therefore, no wife: one worse,
And better us'd, would make her sainted spirit
Again possess her corpse, and on this stage,
Where we offenders now, appear soul-vex'd,
And begin, 'Why to me?'

    Paulina.   Had she such power,   60
She had just cause.

Leontes. She had; and would incense me
To murther her I married.

Paulina. I should so.
Were I the ghost that walk'd, I'd bid you mark
Her eye, and tell me for what dull part in 't
You chose her; then I'd shriek, that even your ears
Should rift to hear me; and the words that follow'd
Should be ' Remember mine.'

Leontes. Stars, stars,
And all eyes else dead coals !—Fear thou no wife;
I 'll have no wife, Paulina.

Paulina. Will you swear
Never to marry but by my free leave ?

Leontes. Never, Paulina ! so be blest my spirit !

Paulina. Then, good my lords, bear witness to his oath.

Cleomenes. You tempt him over-much.

Paulina. Unless another,
As like Hermione as is her picture,
Affront his eye.

Cleomenes. Good madam,—

Paulina. I have done.
Yet, if my lord will marry,—if you will, sir,
No remedy, but you will,—give me the office
To choose you a queen. She shall not be so young
As was your former; but she shall be such
As, walk'd your first queen's ghost, it should take joy
To see her in your arms.

Leontes. My true Paulina,
We shall not marry till thou bid'st us.

Paulina. That
Shall be when your first queen 's again in breath;
Never till then.

Enter a Gentleman.

Gentleman. One that gives out himself Prince Florizel,

Son of Polixenes, with his princess,—she
The fairest I have yet beheld,—desires access
To your high presence.

    Leontes.   What with him? he comes not
Like to his father's greatness; his approach,
So out of circumstance and sudden, tells us   90
'T is not a visitation fram'd, but forc'd
By need and accident.   What train?

    Gentleman.   But few,
And those but mean.

    Leontes.   His princess, say you, with him?

    Gentleman. Ay, the most peerless piece of earth, I think,
That e'er the sun shone bright on.

    Paulina.   O Hermione,
As every present time doth boast itself
Above a better gone, so must thy grave
Give way to what 's seen now!—Sir, you yourself
Have said and writ so, but your writing now
Is colder than that theme, 'She had not been,   100
Nor was not to be equall'd;'—thus your verse
Flow'd with her beauty once: 't is shrewdly ebb'd,
To say you have seen a better.

    Gentleman.   Pardon, madam:
The one I have almost forgot,—your pardon,—
The other, when she has obtain'd your eye,
Will have your tongue too.   This is a creature,
Would she begin a sect, might quench the zeal
Of all professors else, make proselytes
Of who she but bid follow.

    Paulina.   How! not women?

    Gentleman. Women will love her, that she is a woman
More worth than any man; men, that she is   111
The rarest of all women.

    Leontes.   Go, Cleomenes;
Yourself, assisted with your honour'd friends,

Bring them to our embracement.—Still, 't is strange
                    [*Exeunt Cleomenes and others.*
He thus should steal upon us.
    Paulina.   Had our prince,
Jewel of children, seen this hour, he had pair'd
Well with this lord; there was not full a month
Between their births.
    Leontes.   Prithee, no more; cease; thou know'st
He dies to me again when talk'd of: sure,
When I shall see this gentleman, thy speeches   120
Will bring me to consider that which may
Unfurnish me of reason.—They are come.—

Re-enter CLEOMENES *and others,* with FLORIZEL *and* PERDITA.

Your mother was most true to wedlock, prince;
For she did print your royal father off,
Conceiving you.   Were I but twenty-one,
Your father's image is so hit in you,
His very air, that I should call you brother,
As I did him, and speak of something wildly
By us perform'd before.   Most dearly welcome!
And your fair princess,—goddess!—O, alas!   130
I lost a couple, that 'twixt heaven and earth
Might thus have stood begetting wonder as
You, gracious couple, do; and then I lost—
All mine own folly—the society,
Amity too, of your brave father, whom,
Though bearing misery, I desire my life
Once more to look on him.
    Florizel.   By his command
Have I here touch'd Sicilia, and from him
Give you all greetings that a king, at friend,
Can send his brother: and, but infirmity   140
Which waits upon worn times hath something seiz'd
His wish'd ability, he had himself
                   I

The lands and waters 'twixt your throne and his
Measur'd to look upon you; whom he loves—
He bade me say so—more than all the sceptres
And those that bear them living.

    Leontes.   O my brother,
Good gentleman! the wrongs I have done thee stir
Afresh within me, and these thy offices,
So rarely kind, are as interpreters
Of my behind-hand slackness.—Welcome hither,   150
As is the spring to the earth. And hath he too
Expos'd this paragon to the fearful usage,
At least ungentle, of the dreadful Neptune,
To greet a man not worth her pains, much less
The adventure of her person?

    Florizel.   Good my lord,
She came from Libya.

    Leontes.   Where the warlike Smalus,
That noble honour'd lord, is fear'd and lov'd?

    Florizel. Most royal sir, from thence; from him, whose
         daughter
His tears proclaim'd his, parting with her: thence,
A prosperous south-wind friendly, we have cross'd,   160
To execute the charge my father gave me
For visiting your highness. My best train
I have from your Sicilian shores dismiss'd;
Who for Bohemia bend, to signify
Not only my success in Libya, sir,
But my arrival and my wife's in safety
Here where we are.

    Leontes.   The blessed gods
Purge all infection from our air whilst you
Do climate here! You have a holy father,
A graceful gentleman; against whose person,   170
So sacred as it is, I have done sin:
For which the heavens, taking angry note,

Have left me issueless; and your father's blest,
As he from heaven merits it, with you
Worthy his goodness. What might I have been,
Might I a son and daughter now have look'd on,
Such goodly things as you!

Enter a Lord.

 Lord.   Most noble sir,
That which I shall report will bear no credit,
Were not the proof so nigh. Please you, great sir,
Bohemia greets you from himself by me;   180
Desires you to attach his son, who has—
His dignity and duty both cast off—
Fled from his father, from his hopes, and with
A shepherd's daughter.
 Leontes.   Where's Bohemia? speak.
 Lord. Here in your city; I now came from him.
I speak amazedly; and it becomes
My marvel and my message. To your court
Whiles he was hastening, in the chase, it seems,
Of this fair couple, meets he on the way
The father of this seeming lady and   190
Her brother, having both their country quitted
With this young prince.
 Florizel.   Camillo has betray'd me;
Whose honour and whose honesty till now
Endur'd all weathers.
 Lord.   Lay 't so to his charge;
He's with the king your father.
 Leontes.   Who? Camillo?
 Lord. Camillo, sir; I spake with him; who now
Has these poor men in question. Never saw I
Wretches so quake; they kneel, they kiss the earth,
Forswear themselves as often as they speak:
Bohemia stops his ears, and threatens them
With divers deaths in death.

Perdita.   O my poor father !—
The heaven sets spies upon us, will not have
Our contract celebrated.

   Leontes.   You are married ?

   Florizel. We are not, sir, nor are we like to be;
The stars, I see, will kiss the valleys first :
The odds for high and low 's alike.

   Leontes.   My lord,
Is this the daughter of a king ?

   Florizel.   She is,
When once she is my wife.

   Leontes. That once, I see by your good father's speed,
Will come on very slowly.   I am sorry,   210
Most sorry, you have broken from his liking
Where you were tied in duty, and as sorry
Your choice is not so rich in worth as beauty,
That you might well enjoy her.

   Florizel.   Dear, look up :
Though Fortune, visible an enemy,
Should chase us with my father, power no jot
Hath she to change our loves.—Beseech you, sir,
Remember since you owed no more to time
Than I do now : with thought of such affections,
Step forth mine advocate ; at your request   220
My father will grant precious things as trifles.

   Leontes. Would he do so, I 'd beg your precious mistress,
Which he counts but a trifle.

   Paulina.   Sir, my liege,
Your eye hath too much youth in 't; not a month
Fore your queen died, she was more worth such gazes
Than what you look on now.

   Leontes.   I thought of her,
Even in these looks I made.—[*To Florizel*] But your peti-
     tion
Is yet unanswer'd.   I will to your father.

Your honour not o'erthrown by your desires,
I am friend to them and you : upon which errand　　230
I now go toward him ; therefore follow me
And mark what way I make.　Come, good my lord.

[Exeunt.

SCENE II.　*Before the Palace of Leontes.*

Enter AUTOLYCUS *and a* Gentleman.

Autolycus. Beseech you, sir, were you present at this relation ?

1 *Gentleman.* I was by at the opening of the fardel,
heard the old shepherd deliver the manner how he found
it : whereupon, after a little amazedness, we were all commanded out of the chamber ; only this methought I heard
the shepherd say, he found the child.

Autolycus. I would most gladly know the issue of it.　　8

1 *Gentleman.* I make a broken delivery of the business ;
but the changes I perceived in the king and Camillo were
very notes of admiration.　They seemed almost, with star-
ing on one another, to tear the cases of their eyes ; there
was speech in their dumbness, language in their very gest-
ure ; they looked as they had heard of a world ransomed,
or one destroyed.　A notable passion of wonder appeared
in them ; but the wisest beholder, that knew no more but
seeing, could not say if the importance were joy or sorrow ;
but in the extremity of the one, it must needs be.—

Enter another Gentleman.

Here comes a gentleman that happily knows more.—The
news, Rogero ?　　20

2 *Gentleman.* Nothing but bonfires.　The oracle is fulfilled ; the king's daughter is found.　Such a deal of won
der is broken out within this hour that ballad-makers can
not be able to express it.

Enter a third Gentleman.

Here comes the Lady Paulina's steward; he can deliver you more.—How goes it now, sir? this news which is called true is so like an old tale, that the verity of it is in strong suspicion.   Has the king found his heir?   28

   3 *Gentleman.* Most true, if ever truth were pregnant by circumstance; that which you hear you 'll swear you see, there is such unity in the proofs.   The mantle of Queen Hermione's, her jewel about the neck of it, the letters of Antigonus found with it which they know to be his character, the majesty of the creature in resemblance of the mother, the affection of nobleness which nature shows above her breeding, and many other evidences proclaim her with all certainty to be the king's daughter.   Did you see the meeting of the two kings?

   2 *Gentleman.* No.   39

   3 *Gentleman.* Then have you lost a sight, which was to be seen, cannot be spoken of.   There might you have beheld one joy crown another, so and in such manner that it seemed sorrow wept to take leave of them, for their joy waded in tears.   There was casting up of eyes, holding up of hands, with countenances of such distraction that they were to be known by garment, not by favour.   Our king, being ready to leap out of himself for joy of his found daughter, as if that joy were now become a loss, cries ' O, thy mother, thy mother!' then asks Bohemia forgiveness; then embraces his son-in-law; then again worries he his daughter with clipping her; now he thanks the old shepherd, which stands by like a weather-bitten conduit of many kings' reigns.   I never heard of such another encounter, which lames report to follow it and undoes description to do it.   55

   2 *Gentleman.* What, pray you, became of Antigonus, that carried hence the child?

3 *Gentleman.* Like an old tale still, which will have matter to rehearse, though credit be asleep and not an ear open. He was torn to pieces with a bear: this avouches the shepherd's son; who has not only his innocence, which seems much, to justify him, but a handkerchief and rings of his that Paulina knows.

1 *Gentleman.* What became of his bark and his followers?   65

3 *Gentleman.* Wracked the same instant of their master's death, and in the view of the shepherd; so that all the instruments which aided to expose the child were even then lost when it was found. But O, the noble combat that 'twixt joy and sorrow was fought in Paulina! She had one eye declined for the loss of her husband, another elevated that the oracle was fulfilled; she lifted the princess from the earth, and so locks her in embracing, as if she would pin her to her heart that she might no more be in danger of losing.

1 *Gentleman.* The dignity of this act was worth the audience of kings and princes; for by such was it acted.   77

3 *Gentleman.* One of the prettiest touches of all and that which angled for mine eyes, caught the water though not the fish, was when, at the relation of the queen's death, with the manner how she came to 't bravely confessed and lamented by the king, how attentiveness wounded his daughter; till, from one sign of dolour to another, she did, with an 'Alas,' I would fain say, bleed tears, for I am sure my heart wept blood. Who was most marble there changed colour; some swooned, all sorrowed: if all the world could have seen 't, the woe had been universal.

1 *Gentleman.* Are they returned to the court?   88

3 *Gentleman.* No: the princess hearing of her mother's statue, which is in the keeping of Paulina,—a piece many years in doing and now newly performed by that rare Italian master, Julio Romano, who, had he himself eternity and

could put breath into his work, would beguile Nature of her custom, so perfectly he is her ape;—he so near to Hermione hath done Hermione that they say one would speak to her and stand in hope of answer:—thither with all greediness of affection are they gone, and there they intend to sup.   98

2 *Gentleman.* I thought she had some great matter there in hand; for she hath privately twice or thrice a day, ever since the death of Hermione, visited that removed house. Shall we thither and with our company piece the rejoicing?

1 *Gentleman.* Who would be thence that has the benefit of access? every wink of an eye some new grace will be born; our absence makes us unthrifty to our knowledge. Let 's along.   [*Exeunt Gentlemen.*

Autolycus. Now, had I not the dash of my former life in me, would preferment drop on my head. I brought the old man and his son aboard the prince; told him I heard them talk of a fardel and I know not what: but he at that time, overfond of the shepherd's daughter, so he then took her to be, who began to be much sea-sick, and himself little better, extremity of weather continuing, this mystery remained undiscovered. But 't is all one to me; for had I been the finder-out of this secret, it would not have relished among my other discredits.—   117

Enter Shepherd *and* Clown.

Here come those I have done good to against my will, and already appearing in the blossoms of their fortune.

Shepherd. Come, boy; I am past moe children, but thy sons and daughters will be all gentlemen born.

Clown. You are well met, sir. You denied to fight with me this other day, because I was no gentleman born. See you these clothes? say you see them not and think me still no gentleman born; you were best say these robes are not

gentlemen born : give me the lie, do, and try whether I am
not now a gentleman born.

Autolycus. I know you are now, sir, a gentleman born.

Clown. Ay, and have been so any time these four hours.

Shepherd. And so have I, boy.   130

Clown. So you have : but I was a gentleman born before
my father : for the king's son took me by the hand, and
called me brother ; and then the two kings called my father brother ; and then the prince my brother and the princess my sister called my father father ; and so we wept,
and there was the first gentleman-like tears that ever we
shed.

Shepherd. We may live, son, to shed many more.

Clown. Ay ; or else 't were hard luck, being in so preposterous estate as we are.   140

Autolycus. I humbly beseech you, sir, to pardon me all
the faults I have committed to your worship and to give me
your good report to the prince my master.

Shepherd. Prithee, son, do ; for we must be gentle, now
we are gentlemen.

Clown. Thou wilt amend thy life?

Autolycus. Ay, an it like your good worship.

Clown. Give me thy hand ; I will swear to the prince
thou art as honest a true fellow as any is in Bohemia.

Shepherd. You may say it, but not swear it.   150

Clown. Not swear it, now I am a gentleman ? Let boors
and franklins say it, I 'll swear it.

Shepherd. How if it be false, son?

Clown. If it be ne'er so false, a true gentleman may
swear it in the behalf of his friend : and I 'll swear to the
prince thou art a tall fellow of thy hands and that thou
wilt not be drunk ; but I know thou art no tall fellow of
thy hands and that thou wilt be drunk : but I 'll swear it,
and I would thou wouldst be a tall fellow of thy hands.

Autolycus. I will prove so, sir, to my power.   16

Clown. Ay, by any means prove a tall fellow; if I do
not wonder how thou darest venture to be drunk, not being a tall fellow, trust me not.—Hark! the kings and the
princes, our kindred, are going to see the queen's picture.
Come, follow us; we'll be thy good masters.   [*Exeunt.*

SCENE III.   *A Chapel in Paulina's House.*

Enter LEONTES, POLIXENES, FLORIZEL, PERDITA, CAMILLO,
    PAULINA, Lords, *and* Attendants.

Leontes. O grave and good Paulina, the great comfort
That I have had of thee!
Paulina.   What, sovereign sir,
I did not well I meant well.   All my services
You have paid home; but that you have vouchsaf'd,
With your crown'd brother and these your contracted
Heirs of your kingdoms, my poor house to visit,
It is a surplus of your grace, which never
My life may last to answer.
Leontes.   O Paulina,
We honour you with trouble: but we came
To see the statue of our queen; your gallery   10
Have we pass'd through, not without much content
In many singularities, but we saw not
That which my daughter came to look upon,
The statue of her mother.
Paulina.   As she liv'd peerless,
So her dead likeness, I do well believe,
Excels whatever yet you look'd upon
Or hand of man hath done; therefore I keep it
Lonely, apart.   But here it is; prepare
To see the life as lively mock'd as ever
Still sleep mock'd death.   Behold, and say 't is well.   20
    [*Paulina draws a curtain, and discovers Hermione
        standing like a statue.*

I like your silence, it the more shows off
Your wonder: but yet speak; first, you, my liege.
Comes it not something near?

 Leontes.   Her natural posture!—
Chide me, dear stone, that I may say indeed
Thou art Hermione; or rather, thou art she
In thy not chiding, for she was as tender
As infancy and grace.—But yet, Paulina,
Hermione was not so much wrinkled, nothing
So aged as this seems.

 Polixenes.   O, not by much!

 Paulina. So much the more our carver's excellence; **30**
Which lets go by some sixteen years, and makes her
As she liv'd now.

 Leontes.   As now she might have done,
So much to my good comfort, as it is
Now piercing to my soul. O, thus she stood,
Even with such life of majesty, warm life,
As now it coldly stands, when first I woo'd her!
I am asham'd; does not the stone rebuke me
For being more stone than it?—O royal piece!
There's magic in thy majesty, which has
My evils conjur'd to remembrance, and **40**
From thy admiring daughter took the spirits,
Standing like stone with thee.

 Perdita.   And give me leave,
And do not say 't is superstition, that
I kneel and then implore her blessing.—Lady,
Dear queen, that ended when I but began,
Give me that hand of yours to kiss.

 Paulina.   O, patience!
The statue is but newly fix'd, the colour's
Not dry.

 Camillo. My lord, your sorrow was too sore laid on,
Which sixteen winters cannot blow away, **50**

So many summers dry : scarce any joy
Did ever so long live ; no sorrow
But kill'd itself much sooner.

    Polixenes.   Dear my brother
Let him that was the cause of this have power
To take off so much grief from you as he
Will piece up in himself.

    Paulina.   Indeed, my lord,
If I had thought the sight of my poor image
Would thus have wrought you,—for the stone is mine—
I 'd not have show'd it.

    Leontes.   Do not draw the curtain.

    Paulina. No longer shall you gaze on 't, lest your fancy
May think anon it moves.

    Leontes.   Let be, let be.
Would I were dead, but that, methinks, already—
What was he that did make it?—See, my lord,
Would you not deem it breath'd ? and that those veins
Did verily bear blood ?

    Polixenes.   Masterly done ;
The very life seems warm upon her lip.

    Leontes. The fixure of her eye has motion in 't,
As we are mock'd with art.

    Paulina.   I 'll draw the curtain ;
My lord 's almost so far transported that
He 'll think anon it lives.

    Leontes.   O sweet Paulina,
Make me to think so twenty years together !
No settled senses of the world can match
The pleasure of that madness.   Let 't alone.

    Paulina. I am sorry, sir, I have thus far stirr'd you ; but
I could afflict you farther.

    Leontes.   Do, Paulina ;
For this affliction has a taste as sweet
As any cordial comfort.   Still, methinks,

There is an air comes from her; what fine chisel
Could ever yet cut breath?   Let no man mock me,
For I will kiss her.

   Paulina.   Good my lord, forbear!   80
The ruddiness upon her lip is wet;
You 'll mar it if you kiss it, stain your own
With oily painting.   Shall I draw the curtain?

   Leontes. No, not these twenty years.

   Perdita.   So long could I
Stand by, a looker-on.

   Paulina.   Either forbear,
Quit presently the chapel, or resolve you
For more amazement.   If you can behold it,
I 'll make the statue move indeed, descend
And take you by the hand; but then you 'll think—
Which I protest against—I am assisted   90
By wicked powers.

   Leontes.   What you can make her do,
I am content to look on; what to speak,
I am content to hear; for 't is as easy
To make her speak as move.

   Paulina.   It is requir'd
You do awake your faith.   Then all stand still;
Or those that think it is unlawful business
I am about, let them depart.

   Leontes.   Proceed;
No foot shall stir.

   Paulina.   Music, awake her; strike!—   *[Music.*
'T is time; descend; be stone no more; approach:
Strike all that look upon with marvel.   Come,   100
I 'll fill your grave up; stir, nay, come away,
Bequeath to death your numbness, for from him
Dear life redeems you.—You perceive she stirs.

                          [Hermione comes down.

Start not; her actions shall be holy as
You hear my spell is lawful.   Do not shun her
Until you see her die again; for then
You kill her double.   Nay, present your hand:
When she was young you woo'd her; now in age
Is she become the suitor?

    Leontes.   O, she 's warm!
If this be magic, let it be an art   110
Lawful as eating.

    Polixenes.   She embraces him.

    Camillo. She hangs about his neck;
If she pertain to life, let her speak too.

    Polixenes. Ay, and make 't manifest where she has liv'd,
Or how stolen from the dead.

    Paulina.   That she is living,
Were it but told you, should be hooted at
Like an old tale; but it appears she lives,
Though yet she speak not.   Mark a little while.—
Please you to interpose, fair madam; kneel
And pray your mother's blessing.—Turn, good lady;   120
Our Perdita is found.

    Hermione.   You gods, look down
And from your sacred vials pour your graces
Upon my daughter's head!—Tell me, mine own,
Where hast thou been preserv'd? where liv'd? how found
Thy father's court? for thou shalt hear that I,
Knowing by Paulina that the oracle
Gave hope thou wast in being, have preserv'd
Myself to see the issue.

    Paulina.   There 's time enough for that;
Lest they desire upon this push to trouble
Your joys with like relation.—Go together,   130
You precious winners all; your exultation
Partake to every one.   I, an old turtle,(dove)
Will wing me to some wither'd bough, and there

My mate, that 's never to be found again,
Lament till I am lost.

    Leontes.   O, peace, Paulina!
Thou shouldst a husband take by my consent,
As I by thine a wife; this is a match,
And made between 's by vows. Thou hast found mine;
But how, is to be question'd; for I saw her,
As I thought, dead, and have in vain said many
A prayer upon her grave. I 'll not seek far—
For him, I partly know his mind—to find thee
An honourable husband.—Come, Camillo,
And take her by the hand, whose worth and honesty
Is richly noted and here justified
By us, a pair of kings.—Let 's from this place.—
What! look upon my brother.—Both your pardons,
That e'er I put between your holy looks
My ill suspicion. This is your son-in-law
And son unto the king, whom heavens directing,   150
Is troth-plight to your daughter.—Good Paulina,
Lead us from hence, where we may leisurely
Each one demand and answer to his part
Perform'd in this wide gap of time since first
We were dissever'd. Hastily lead away.   [*Exeunt.*

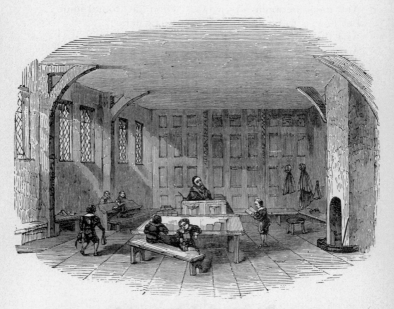

INTERIOR OF GRAMMAR SCHOOL, STRATFORD.

NOTES.

ABBREVIATIONS USED IN THE NOTES.

Abbott (or Gr.), Abbott's *Shakespearian Grammar* (third edition).

A. S., Anglo-Saxon.

A. V., Authorized Version of the Bible (1611).

B. and F., Beaumont and Fletcher.

B. J., Ben Jonson.

Camb. ed., "Cambridge edition" of *Shakespeare*, edited by Clark and Wright.

Cf. (*confer*), compare.

Clarke, "Cassell's Illustrated Shakespeare," edited by Charles and Mary Cowden Clarke (London, n. d.).

Coll., Collier (second edition).

Coll. MS., Manuscript Corrections of Second Folio, edited by Collier.

D., Dyce (second edition).

H., Hudson (first edition).

Halliwell, J. O. Halliwell (folio ed. of Shakespeare).

Id. (*idem*), the same.

K., Knight (second edition).

Nares, *Glossary*, edited by Halliwell and Wright (London, 1859).

Prol., Prologue.

S., Shakespeare.

Schmidt, A. Schmidt's *Shakespeare-Lexicon* (Berlin, 1874).

Sr., Singer.

St., Staunton

Theo., Theobald.

V., Verplanck.

W., White.

Walker, Wm. Sidney Walker's *Critical Examination of the Text of Shakespeare* (London, 1860).

Warb., Warburton.

Wb., Webster's Dictionary (revised quarto edition of 1864).

Worc., Worcester's Dictionary (quarto edition).

The abbreviations of the names of Shakespeare's Plays will be readily understood; as *T. N.* for *Twelfth Night*, *Cor.* for *Coriolanus*, 3 *Hen. VI.* for *The Third Part of King Henry the Sixth*, etc. *P. P.* refers to *The Passionate Pilgrim*; *V. and A.* to *Venus and Adonis*; *L. C.* to *Lover's Complaint*; and *Sonn.* to the *Sonnets*.

When the abbreviation of the name of a play is followed by a reference to *page*, Rolfe's edition of the play is meant.

The numbers of the lines (except for *The Winter's Tale*) are those of the "Globe" ed. or of Crowell's reprint of that ed.

NOTES.

DELPHI AND MOUNT PARNASSUS.

ACT I.

DRAMATIS PERSONÆ.—The folio has the following list at the end of the play (cf. *Oth.* p. 154):

The Names of the Actors.

Leontes, King of Sicillia.
Mamillus, yong Prince of Sicillia.
Camillo.
Antigonus. ⎫ *Foure*
Cleomines. ⎬ *Lords of Sicillia.*
Dion. ⎭
Hermione, Queene to Leontes.
Perdita, Daughter to Leontes and Hermione.
Paulina, wife to Antigonus.

Emilia, a Lady.
Polixenes, King of Bohemia.
Florizell, Prince of Bohemia.
Old Shepheard, reputed Father of Perdita.
Clowne, his Sonne.
Autolicus, a Rogue.
Archidamus, a Lord of Bohemia.
Other Lords, and Gentlemen, and Seruants.
Shepheards, and Shephearddesses.

Scene I.—6. *Bohemia.* The King of Bohemia. See *Macb.* p. 239, or *Hen. V.* p. 159.

Hanmer changed *Bohemia* throughout to "Bithynia;" but, as stated above (see p. 17), S. followed Greene in making Bohemia a maritime country. Farmer remarks: "Corporal Trim's King of Bohemia 'delighted in navigation, and had never a seaport in his dominions;' and my Lord Herbert informs us that De Luines, the prime minister of France, when he was ambassador there, demanded whether Bohemia was an inland country, or 'lay upon the sea.' There is a similar mistake in *T. G. of V.* relative to that city [Verona] and Milan."

Visitation. Cf. iv. 4. 544 and v. 1. 90 below. S. does not use *visit* as a noun. *Visitings* occurs in *Macb.* i. 5. 46.

8. *Wherein*, etc. "Though we cannot give you equal entertainment, yet the consciousness of our good-will shall justify us" (Johnson).

11. *In the freedom of my knowledge.* As my knowledge makes me free to do, or gives me the right to do. Cf. *Sonn.* 46. 4: "the freedom of that right."

14. *Unintelligent.* Unconscious, not aware; used by S. only here.

22. *Such . . . which.* Cf. iv. 4. 738 below: "such secrets in this fardel or box, which none must know," etc. Gr. 278.

25. *Encounters.* Meetings; as often. See *Much Ado,* p. 154.

Hath. The later folios have "have." Abbott (Gr. 334) explains it as the old "third person plural in *th.*" Cf. *R. and J.* prol. 8:

> "Whose misadventur'd piteous overthrows
> Doth with their death bury their parents' strife;"

and see note in our ed. p. 140. We have another instance in **i. 2. 1** below; but that is perhaps to be explained by the interposition of *star.*

Royally attorneyed. "Nobly supplied by substitution of embassies, etc." (Johnson); or "performed by proxy" (Schmidt). In the only other instance of *attorneyed* in S. (*M. for M.* v. i. 390) it is=employed as an attorney.

27. *That. So* that; a common ellipsis. Gr. 283. The Coll. MS. needlessly inserts "so" before *royally.*

28. *A vast.* The later folios have "a vast sea." Cf. *Per.* iii. 1. 1: "Thou god of this great vast, rebuke these surges." See also *Ham.* p. 186.

30. *Loves.* For the plural, see *Macb.* p. 209 or *Ham.* p. 177. Cf. *peaces* in ii. 1. 135 below.

32. *Of.* See Gr. 172.

33. *It is.* Cf. *Macb.* i. 4. 58: "It is a peerless kinsman," etc. It is oftener contemptuous; as in *R. and J.* iv. 2. 14, *A. and C.* iii. 2. 6, etc.

34. *Into my note.* To my knowledge. Cf. *T. N.* iv. 3. 29: "it shall come to note," etc.

36. *Physics the subject.* "Affords a cordial to the state" (Johnson). Cf. *Cymb.* iii. 2. 34: "it doth physic love" (that is, preserve its health). For the collective use of *subject* (=people), see *Ham.* p. 173.

Scene II.—1. *The watery star.* The "watery moon" of *M. N. D.*

ii. 1. 162 (cf. iii. i. 203) and *Rich. III.* ii. 2. 69. See also *R. and J.* i. 4. 62 : "the moonshine's watery beams." For *hath*, see on i. 1. 25 above.

2. *Note.* Means of *noting* or marking time. Cf. *Much Ado*, p. 144. Clarke explains *the shepherd's note* as "noted by the shepherd." "The allusion is peculiarly happy, *shepherds* 'keeping watch of their flocks by *night*' being natural astronomers. Cf. *Luke*, ii. 8" (Crosby).

5. *For perpetuity.* For all time, forever. Cf. *Cymb.* v. 4. 6 : "Groan so in perpetuity," etc.

6. *Like a cipher*, etc. Cf. *Hen. V.* prol. 17 :

> "O pardon ! since a crooked figure may
> Attest in little place a million ;
> And let us, cipners to this great accompt,
> On your imaginary forces work."

8. *Moe.* Changed by most editors to "more." See *A. Y. L.* p. 176.

10. *Part.* Depart. See *M. of V.* p. 145.

12. *That may blow*, etc. O that no nipping winds at home may blow, to make me say, This fear was too well-founded ! For the ellipsis of *O*, Farmer compares an old translation of the *Alcoran* of the Franciscans : "St. Francis . . . said to the priors, That I had a wood of such Junipers !" and *The Two Noble Kinsmen :* "That I, poor man, might eftsoons come between !" Abbott (Gr. 425) explains the passage thus : "I am question'd by my fears . . . that (there) may blow," etc. D. believes the passage to be corrupt. Hanmer changed *No* to "Some" and *truly* to "early" (Capell "tardily ") ; and Warb. *that may* to "may there."

For *sneaping* (=snipping, or nipping), cf. *L. L. L.* i. 1. 100 : "an envious sneaping frost ;" and *R. of L.* 333 : "the sneaped birds."

16. *Put us to 't.* Bring us to it (that is, being tired of you). Cf. iv. 4. 153 below : "put you to 't" (that is, fear).

17. *Seven-night.* Cf. *Much Ado*, ii. 1. 375 : "a just seven-night." See also *A. Y. L.* p. 177, note on *A se'nnight*.

Very sooth. In very sooth, or truth. See *M. of V.* p. 127 and *M. N. D.* p. 153, note on *Good troth*.

18. *Between's.* As Clarke notes, this particular elision, *'s* for *us*, occurs often in this play ; and it is curious to observe how some one peculiarity will recur in certain of Shakespeare's plays, as if he thought in that special way at that special time of writing. For *part*=divide, see *J. C.* p. 186, note on *Part the glories*.

20. *None, none.* "Shakespeare, like a true poet, knew perfectly the potent effect of an iterated word ; but, also like a true poet and writer of thorough judgment, used it but sparingly, and of course, on that account, with redoubled force of impression. Here it has the effect of intense earnestness " (Clarke).

31. *This satisfaction*, etc. "We had satisfactory accounts yesterday of the state of Bohemia " (Johnson).

33. *Ward.* Point of defence ; a metaphor taken from fencing. For the literal use, see *Temp.* i. 2. 471 : "Come from thy ward," etc.

38. *Adventure.* Venture ; as in ii. 3. 162 and iv. 4. 448 below.

39. *Borrow.* S. does not elsewhere use *borrow* as a noun, nor *at* with the name of a country.

41. *Let him there.* "Let him remain there" (Schmidt). Warb. took *let* to be=hinder (cf. *Ham.* i. 4. 85, etc.), and therefore changed *him* in 40 to "you." Clarke adopts Malone's explanation of *let him :* "let or hinder himself," that is, stay.

Gest. The name given to the list (Fr. *giste* or *gîte*) of the appointed stages in a royal progress or journey ; here = the fixed limit of the visit, as the context shows. Steevens cites Strype's *Memorials,* etc., where the Archbishop entreats Cecil "to let him have the new resolved upon gests, from that time to the end, that he might from time to time know where the king was ;" also *Friar Bacon and Friar Bungay,* 1594 :

> "Castile, and lovely Elinor with him,
> Have in their gests resolv'd for Oxford town ;"

and the *The White Devil,* 1612 :

> "like the gests in the progress,
> You know where you shall find me."

The *gests* were strictly the stopping-places, but the name came to be applied to the written list of them.

42. *Good deed.* In very deed ; the *good* being intensive, as in *good sooth* (*Temp.* ii. 2. 150), *good troth* (see on 17 above), etc. The 1st folio has "(good-deed)" here, the later folios have "(good-heed)" or "(good heed)."

43. *Jar.* Tick. Cf. the verb in *Rich. II.* v. 5. 51 :

> "My thoughts are minutes; and with sighs they jar
> Their watches on unto mine eyes," etc.

Holt White quotes Heywood, *Troia Britannica :* "He hears no waking-clocke, nor watch to jarre ;" and Malone adds *The Spanish Tragedy :* "the minutes jerring, and the clocke striking."

44. *What lady she.* Whatever lady she may be, any lady whatever. The Coll. MS. has "should" for *she,* and St. and Abbott (Gr. 255) print "lady-she." Schmidt puts the passage under "*she* = woman" (see *A. Y. L.* p. 170, or Gr. 224), and makes the phrase = "a woman that is a lady ;" but it seems better to consider it elliptical, as W., Clarke, and others do. W. remarks that, while "should" is plausible, the original reading is "neither obscure nor inelegant" and "has a quaint fascination, which is lost in the proposed emendation." Mr. J. Crosby has suggested "e'er" for *she,* but now prefers the latter.

47. *Limber.* Flexible, weak ; the only instance of the word in S.

48. *Unsphere the stars.* Remove them from their *spheres* (as the word was used in the Ptolemaic astronomy) or their orbits. Cf. *M. N. D.* ii. 1. 153 : "And certain stars shot madly from their spheres," etc.

50. *Verily is.* The 1st folio has "Verely ' is ;" and St. and W. read "Verily 's."

53. *Pay your fees,* etc. "An allusion to a piece of English law procedure, which, although it may have been enforced till very recently, could hardly be known to any except lawyers, or those who had themselves actually been in prison on a criminal charge—that, whether guilty or innocent, the prisoner was liable to pay a fee on his liberation" (Lord Campbell).

57. *Should.* For Shakespeare's use of *may, might, shall, should, will, would,* etc., the reader may consult Gr. 307-331.

62. *Lordings.* Lordlings (not used by S.). The word is=lord, in *2 Hen. VI.* i. 1. 145 : " Lordings, farewell ;" and *P. P.* 211 : " It was a lording's daughter, the fairest one of three." Cf. Spenser, *F. Q.* iii. 9. 3 : "Then listen, Lordings," etc.

68. *Chang'd.* Exchanged ; as in *Temp.* i. 2. 441 : " They have chang'd eyes," etc.

70. *Doctrine.* Teaching, instruction. See *R. and J.* p. 146, note on *Pay that doctrine.* Malone made *doctrine* a trisyllable, but that is not satisfactory here. Abbott (Gr. 505) puts the line among those " with four accents." The later folios have " no nor dream'd," and Spedding conjectures " neither dream'd."

73. *Blood.* Passions. See *Much Ado*, p. 131, note on *Faith melteth into blood.*

74. *The imposition clear'd,* etc. " That is, setting aside *original sin ;* bating the imposition from the offence of our first parents, we might have boldly protested our innocence to Heaven " (Warb.).

77. *To 's.* To us. See on 18 above, and cf. 91 and 94 below.

80. *Grace to boot !* " *Grace* or Heaven help me !" (Malone). Cf. *Rich. III.* v. 3. 301 : " Saint George to boot !" which Schmidt thinks may be a parallel case.

84. *And that.* That is, and *if.* See Gr. 285.

86. *Is he won yet ?* Leontes has been aside, playing with Mamillius, while Hermione has been pleading with Polixenes, as he had suggested in 27 above.

87. *At my request he would not.* " Precisely the muttered comment of a susceptible, irritable, jealous-natured man. Be it remarked that Leontes is jealous by nature ; Othello, by circumstance. The one is innately given to suspicion ; the other is with difficulty made suspicious " (Clarke). Cf. p. 31 above.

Gervinus remarks : " Coleridge thought fit to read this play in immediate connection with *Othello,* whose jealousy is in every respect the reverse of that of Leontes. It is so in fact, though we understand the contrast differently from Coleridge. The jealousy of Leontes, and of Othello also, is not founded on the sensitive faculty alone ; in Othello it is deeply connected with his feelings of honour ; in Leontes with tyranny, as Shakespeare says. We should define it more clearly if we were to say with wilfulness. Shakespeare has in both instances shown us the origin of this passion out of a mere nothing, and its frightful consequences ; the destruction of the whole happiness of life in the one, and the happiness of half a life in the other, from the madness of a moment. The pervading difference is that Othello, little disposed to jealousy by nature, is made susceptible of it by circumstances and situations, is driven to it by a cunning whisperer and deceiver ; whereas Leontes, by nature prone to it, has no outward circumstances to induce it, and is his own suggester. The difference of situation in the two is striking : Othello is led to doubt the friend of whom he is jealous by facts not to be denied; he is made to perceive that in his wife her own father had reasons for

being deceived ; the Moor is doubtful of himself and of his own qualities, and he conceives a mistrust of himself and of the world, which was
rooted in his whole situation ; all this heaped together the smouldering
fire of his jealousy, which the false Iago blew into a flame. But Leontes'
situation is quite different : he has no causes of jealousy against his wife,
none against his friend ; his self-reliance, his royal rank, prevent in him
the all-pervading feeling of Othello, who thinks himself despised ; all
those around him, the courtiers, Camillo, Antigonus, Paulina, loudly and
firmly testify against his delusion ; but there is that within himself more
dangerous than the slanderer at Othello's side. After his conscience
has been once infected, after Hermione's friendly invitation and its rejoinder have aroused his suspicion, he is the slave, not of love, not of
passion, not of feeling, but of his own imagination ; dwelling on his own
imaginings, he gives way to the most extraordinary brooding over improbable and impossible things, until he is satisfied of the infallibility of
his convictions, and confirmed in the obstinacy which characterizes the
weak judgment of all wilful persons. This obstinacy, this hard-heartedness, embitters his disposition, and far from feeling, like Othello, pain for
his loss, Leontes indulges in hatred and persecution, and increases both
through his dread of intrigues, which exist only in his own imagination.
The contrast between this wilfulness, this presumed certainty and superior judgment, and the unsuspecting short-sightedness of Othello, is perfect ; and masterly in both is the progress of the delusion, built on quite
different foundations. In contrast with the taciturn Othello, Leontes, in
keeping with his moody and suspicious nature, is a great talker, in whom
thoughts and quick fancies throng, mingle, and pass rapidly from one
object to another."

96. *Heat.* Run, as in a race or *heat.* The Coll. MS. reads "clear,"
and "good" for *goal.* *But to the goal*=but to return to our subject
(dropped at 86 above).

104. *Clap thyself my love.* That is, put your hand in mine, in token of
betrothal. Cf. *T. N.* v. 1. 159 :

> " A contract of eternal bond of love,
>   Confirm'd by mutual joinder of your hands ;"

and see note in our ed. p. 163. See also *M. for M.* v. 1. 209 :

> "This is the hand which, with a vow'd contract,
>   Was fast belock'd in mine ;"

and *K. John,* ii. 1. 532 : " Command thy son and daughter to join hands."
Clap hands was the common expression for pledging faith in this way.
Steevens quotes *Ram Alley,* 1611 :

> " Speak, widow, is 't a match?
>   Shall we clap it up?"

A Trick to Catch the Old One, 1618 : " Come, clap hands, a match !" and
Hen. V. v. 2. 133 : " And so clap hands, and a bargain." Malone adds
from Middleton, *No Wit like a Woman's :* " There these young lovers
shall clap hands together." Rowe (2d ed.) changed *clap* to " clepe "
(=call). See also on iv. 4. 372 below.

105. '*T is.* To mend the metre, Hanmer gave "This is," and Capell "it is."

110. *Tremor cordis.* Trembling of the heart (Latin). *Dances*=throbs.

113. *Bounty's fertile bosom.* Hanmer's emendation of the "bounty, fertile bosom" of the folios. It is generally adopted by the editors.

115. *Paddling palms.* A contemptuous phrase. Cf. *Oth.* ii. 1. 259 : "Didst thou not see her paddle with the palm of his hand?" and *Ham.* iii. 4. 185 : "Or paddling in your neck with his damn'd fingers." S. uses the word only in these passages.

118. *The mort o' the deer.* A prolonged note blown on the horn at the death (Fr. *mort*) of the deer. Steevens quotes Greene, *Card of Fancy :* "He that bloweth the mort before the death of the buck may very well miss of his fees ;" and *Chevy Chace* (earliest form) : "The blewe a mort uppone the bent." Here it probably means the dying gasp of the deer.

119. *Nor my brows.* The allusion is to the horns of the cuckold, as in so many passages that follow. Cf. *Much Ado*, p. 123, notes on *Recheat* and *Baldrick.*

120. *I' fecks !* A corruption of *in faith* (some say of *in fact*). S. uses it only here. Halliwell cites Heywood, *Edward IV.:* "by my feckins !"

121. *Bawcock.* "A term of endearment, synonymous with *chuck* [see *Macb.* p. 212], but always masculine" (Schmidt). Cf. *Hen. V.* iii. 2. 26, iv. 1. 44, and *T. N.* iii. 4. 125.

What, hast smutch'd thy nose ? "It is reserved for such a poet as Shakespeare to fearlessly introduce such natural touches as a flying particle of smut resting upon a child's nose, and to make it turn to wonderfully effective account in stirring a father's heart, agitating it with wild thoughts, and prompting fierce plays upon words and bitter puns. Every phase that passion takes — writhing silence, tortured utterance, tearful lamentations, muttered jests more heart-withering than cries or complaints — all are known to Shakespeare, and are found in his page as in nature's" (Clarke).

123. *Not neat*, etc. "Recollecting that *neat* is the ancient term for *horned* cattle, he says *not neat, but cleanly* " (Johnson).

125. *Virginalling.* Playing with her fingers, as on a *virginal*, a keyed instrument somewhat like a small pianoforte, probably so called because used by young girls (Nares). It was sometimes called *a pair of virginals :* as in Dekker's *Gul's Hornbooke:* "leap up and down like the nimble jacks of a pair of virginals." In like manner an organ was sometimes called *a pair of organs.* Halliwell quotes Middleton, *Chaste Maid*, where the goldsmith's wife says to her daughter : "Moll, have you played over all your old lessons o' the virginals ?"

K. remarks that the idea conveyed in this passage is elaborated in *Sonn.* 128.

128. *Pash.* A word that has puzzled the commentators (see Nares). Jamieson (*Scottish Dict.*) defines it as "head ; a ludicrous term," and marks it as still used in Scotland. *Shoots* = budding horns.

132. *O'er-dyed blacks.* That is, black fabrics *dyed over* with some other colour ; or, possibly, as some explain it, *dyed too much.* Clarke says : "The unsoundness of stuffs subjected to a black dye is notorious, and

renders Shakespeare's simile super-excellent." The Coll. MS. reads
"our dead," and St. conjectures "oft dyed." Steevens remarks that
"black will receive no other hue without discovering itself through it,"
and quotes Pliny, *Hist. Nat.:* "Lanarum nigrae nullum colorem bibunt."
Malone adds Lyly, *Euphues:* "Truly (quoth Camillo) my wool was
blacke, and therefore it would take no other colour."

Halliwell remarks that mourning habiliments were often called *blacks*,
and cites, among other illustrations, a letter dated 1619 : "The queen's
funeral is like to be deferred for want of money to buy the blacks;" and
Heywood, *Eng. Traveller:* "To weare blacks without, but other thoughts
within."

134. *Bourn.* Boundary; as in *Ham.* iii. 1. 79, etc.

136. *Welkin.* Heavenly (Schmidt), or, possibly, blue. See *R. and J.*
p. 172, note on *Grey eye.* See also *M. N. D.* p. 168.

For *villain* as a term of endearment, cf. *C. of E.* i. 2. 19 and *T. A.* v. 1.
30. It is feminine in *T. N.* ii. 5. 16 and *T. and C.* iii. 2. 35.

137. *Dear'st.* For the contraction, see Gr. 473. Cf. iii. 2. 199 below :
"sweet'st, dear'st," etc.

Collop. Part of my own flesh; literally, a slice of meat. Cf. *1 Hen. VI.*
v. 4. 18 : "God knows thou art a collop of my flesh !" Heywood, in his
Epigrams, 1566 (quoted by Boswell), gives it as a proverbial phrase :

> "For I have heard saie it is a deere collup,
> That is cut out of th' owne fleshe."

Can thy dam?—may't be? Can thy mother be guilty of unfaithfulness?
Is it possible? See on iii. 2. 196 below.

138. *Affection ! thy intention,* etc. Schmidt explains this : "Natural
propensity, thy power rules the inmost thoughts of men." *Affection* is
clearly = sensual passion, or lust, as Mr. J. Crosby explains it (*Amer. Bib-
liopolist*, Dec. 1876, p. 121), but we are not so sure that he is right in
making *thy intention stabs the centre* = "thy intensity penetrates to and
pervades every foot of the habitable globe" (cf. *centre* in ii. 1. 98 below).
We rather take it to be = thy aim goes straight to its mark. For the rest
of the passage Mr. Crosby's explanation is perfectly satisfactory : "Continuing his jaundiced ruminations on the *effects of lust,* he says, 'We know
thy pervasive force regards not even impossible things, but overcomes
all obstacles, making them *possible* and subsidiary to thy will. Why, then,
may not my queen, who I could have sworn was purity itself, become corrupt when infected with thy poison?' Another natural fact also strikes
his imagination, 'We know *thou communicat'st with dreams,* though *how
this can be* we are unable to explain. If, then, *with what's unreal thou coactive art,* and in imagination *fellow'st* corporeally *with nothing,* how much
more *credent* (credible) is it that *thou might'st co-join with something !'* . . .
Thus we understand the train of his jealous logic, and see how he works
up his mind to a state of frenzied certainty, when, in conclusion, he ex-
claims, '*Thou dost !* I am satisfied. Thy wicked passion sates itself to
the full, *and that beyond commission*—without *warrant,* or regard to *me,* or
my *authority.* Already I feel the evidence of this fearful power of *affection*—inwardly, in *the infection of my brains,* and outwardly, peering out in
the hardening of my brows.'"

For *credent* = credible, cf. *M. for M.* iv. 4. 29 : "a credent bulk ;" and for *commission* = warrant, cf. 40 above. See also *V. and A.* 568 :

"Things out of hope are compass'd oft with venturing,
Chiefly in love, whose leave exceeds commission," etc.

147. *Something... unsettled.* Somewhat disturbed. For the transposition of the adverbial *something*, cf. 2 *Hen. IV.* i. 2. 212 : "with a white head and something a round belly" (that is, somewhat round).

148. *What cheer*, etc. In the folios this line is given to Leontes ; but it appears to be part of the speech of Polixenes, to whom it was restored by Steevens, at the suggestion of Rann. The emendation is generally adopted by the editors. In the preceding line, St., D., and K. read "Ho" for *How.* K., who follows the folio, says : "Leontes, even in his moody reverie, has his eye fixed upon his queen and Polixenes ; and when he is addressed by the latter with 'Ho ! my lord !' he replies, with a forced gayety, 'What cheer ? how is 't with you?' The addition of 'best brother' is, we apprehend, meant to be uttered in a tone of bitter irony."

149. *Held.* The verb is often, as here = have. Cf. iv. 4. 398 below : "Should hold some counsel," etc. For *brow of much distraction*, cf. v. 2. 45 below : "countenance of such distraction," etc.

151. *It's.* One of the rare instances of the possessive neuter pronoun in S. See *Temp.* p. 120 and *Ham.* p. 186. The word here is spelt "it's" in the folios, as in every other instance except *M. for M.* i. 2. 4, where we find "its." For *it* possessive, see on ii. 3. 178 below. Cf. Gr. 228. *Itself* is printed as two words ("it self") in the folios ; and in *Cymb.* iii. 4. 160 the two are separated by an adjective : "it pretty self."

154. *Methought.* The folios have "me thoughts" ("methoughts" in the 4th); as in *Rich. III.* i. 4. 9, 24. There, by the way, as here, we find in the folio *methought* and *methoughts* mixed up in the same speech. *Methoughts* was a form in use (probably suggested by *methinks*), but here it is probably a misprint, as we have *methought* just below in 159. Coll. adopts the reading of the Egerton MS., "my thoughts." See *M. of V.* p. 135.

158. *Do.* The folios have "do's" or "does." Cf. Gr. 333.

160. *Squash.* An immature peascod. See *M. N. D.* p. 160.

161. *Will you take eggs for money ?* A proverbial expression = will you let yourself be duped or imposed upon, or will you take an affront ? The origin of the phrase has not been satisfactorily made out ; but we find *egg* used to denote something insignificant or worthless in *A. W.* iv. 3. 280 : "He will steal, sir, an egg out of a cloister." According to the Var. of 1821, "Smith" states that the French have a proverb, "A qui vendez-vous coquilles ? that is, whom do you design to affront ?" Steevens quotes *A Match at Midnight*, 1633 : "I shall have eggs for my money ; I must hang myself;" and Reed adds from *Relations of the most famous Kingdomes*, etc., 1630 : "The French infantery skirmisheth bravely afarre off, and cavallery gives a furious onset at the first charge ; but after the first heat they will take eggs for their money" (that is, tamely yield to the attack). The meaning here is sufficiently shown by the reply, *No, my lord, I 'll fight.*

163. *Happy man be 's dole !* "May his *dole* or *share* in life be to be a

happy man!" (Johnson). The expression was proverbial. Cf. *M. W.* iii. 4. 68, *T. of S.* i. 1. 144, and 1 *Hen. IV.* ii. 2. 81. *Dole* was the term (as it still is in England) for a charitable allowance of provision to the poor. Cf. *A. W.* ii. 3. 76 : "what dole of honour" (that is, share, portion) ; and 2 *Hen. IV.* i. 1. 169 : "in the dole of blows" (that is, dealing or giving).

170. *Childness.* "Childishness," which is the word elsewhere used by S. Cf. *Cor.* v. 3. 157, etc.

171. *Thick.* Used by S. only here ; for *thicken*, see *Macb.* p. 212, note on *Light thickens.* Cf. *Macb.* i. 5. 44 : "make thick my blood."

Squire. Here used with half-sportive tenderness. For its contemptuous use, cf. *Much Ado*, i. 3. 54, *Oth.* iv. 2. 145, etc.

172. *Offic'd.* "Having a place or function" (Schmidt). Cf. *Oth.* i. 3. 271 : "My speculative and offic'd instruments" ("active" in the quartos).

174. *How thou lovest us*, etc. "Thus enjoined by himself, it could be only the cruel injustice of that most unjust passion, jealousy, that makes Leontes resent his wife's courtesy to Polixenes as a proof of her guilt" (Clarke).

177. *Apparent.* That is, heir apparent ; as in 3 *Hen. VI.* ii. 2. 64 : "as apparent to the crown."

178. *Shall 's.* Shall us ; that is, shall we. Cf. *Cor.* iv. 6. 148 : "Shall 's to the Capitol ?" See also *T. of A.* iv. 3. 408, *Cymb.* iv. 2. 233, v. 5. 228, *Per.* iv. 5. 7, etc. Gr. 215.

W. remarks : "S. had the minute details of the old novel vividly in mind here : ' When *Pandosto* was busied with such urgent affaires that hee could not bee present with his friend *Egistus, Bellaria* would walke with him into the garden, where they two in privat and pleasant devises would passe away the time to both their contents.' "

179. *To your own bents*, etc. Dispose of yourselves according to your inclination.

181. *How I give iine.* Cf. 2 *Hen. IV.* iv. 4. 39 : "give him line and scope."

183. *Neb.* Beak, here=mouth. Steevens quotes Paynter, *Palace of Pleasure*, 1566 : "the amorous wormes of love did bitterly gnawe and teare his heart wyth the nebs of their forked heads." Rowe changed it to "nib," the more common form of the word. Halliwell quotes Kennett's *Glossary* (MS. Lansd. 1033) : " *Neb*, nose, *Bor. et Kent*, hold up your nebb, Sax. *nebbe*, nasus, nares ; item nostrum,* the bill, beak, nib or nebbe of a bird ; whence, by metaphor, the nib or nebbe of a pen ; Island. *nebbe*, nasus ;" *Two Maids of Moreclacke*, 1609 : "Shal 's not busse, knight ? shal 's not neb ?" and MS. Bodl. 652 : "He kisseth Benjamin, anon his neb he gan wipe."

185. *Allowing.* "Approving" (Malone), or "conniving" (Schmidt).

186. *Fork'd.* Horned. Cf. *Oth.* iii. 3. 276 : "this forked plague" (that is, cuckoldom). See also *T. and C.* i. 2. 178.

188. *So . . . whose.* Cf. *J. C.* i. 2. 316 : "For who so firm that cannot be seduc'd ?" See also *such . . . which* in i. 1. 22 above, and *such . . . that* in 253 below. Gr. 278, 279.

---

* So in Halliwell ; probably a misprint for "rostrum."—*Ed.*

190. *There have been*, etc. Cf. *Oth.* iv. 1. 63 fol.

195. *Strike.* Cf. *Ham.* i. 1. 162 : "no planets strike ;" and see note in our ed. p. 177.

196. *Predominant.* An astrological term. Cf. *A. W.* i. 1. 211 : "When he [Mars] was predominant." See *Macb.* p. 203, note on *Is 't night's predominance*, etc. For *on 's*=of us, see Gr. 182.

198. *They.* Omitted in the 1st folio, but supplied in the 2d.

202. *This great sir.* Cf. iv. 4. 350 : "this ancient sir ;" *T. N.* iii. 4. 81 : "Some sir of note," etc.

204. *Came home.* A nautical phrase=would not hold.

206. *More material.* Either =*the* more important the more you besought him (Clarke), or more urgent than your *petitions*.

207. *They 're here with me*, etc. "They go so far with respect to me as to whisper," etc. (Schmidt) ; or, perhaps, "they are aware of my condition" (V.). For *round*=murmur, whisper, cf. *K. John*, ii. 1. 566 : "rounded in the ear ;" and see *Hen. VIII.* p. 168, foot-note.

208. *So-forth.* Steevens says : "At the corner of Fleet Market, I lately heard one woman, describing another, say 'Everybody knows that her husband is a so-forth.' As she spoke the last word, her fingers expressed the emblem of cuckoldom."

209. *Gust.* Perceive ; literally, taste. Cf. the noun in *Sonn.* 114. 11 and *T. N.* i. 3. 33.

212. *So it is.* We should say, *as* it is.

214. *Thy conceit is soaking*, etc. Thy mind is absorbent, and takes in more than ordinary blockheads do. Clarke sees a metaphorical allusion to the dyeing of hats, indicated by the word *blocks*, which was used for *hats* in that day, and which S. punningly uses for *heads* also : "Was this black aspect of the matter taken by any pate but thine ? For thy conception of it is steeped in the dye, and will draw in more than the ordinary run of hat-heads." For *block*=the wood on which hats were formed, see *Much Ado*, i. 1. 77. In *Lear*, iv. 6. 187 it is = the fashion or form of a hat.

216. *Severals.* Individuals. See *Hen. V.* p. 146.

217. *Lower messes.* Persons of inferior rank, those who sat at the lower end of the table. At a great man's table, the guests were not only seated according to their rank or dignity, but were divided into two grades by the great salt-cellar in the middle of the board. Steevens cites in illustration of this Dekker, *Hon. Wh.:* "Plague him ; set him beneath the salt, and let him not touch a bit till every one has had his full cut ;" and B. and F., *Woman Hater*, i. 2 : "Uncut-up pies at the nether end, filled with moss and stones, partly to make a shew with, and partly to keep the lower mess from eating." "In the *Northumberland Household Booke* we find that the clerks of the kitchen are to be with the cooks at the 'striking out of the messes ;' and in the same curious picture of ancient manners there are the most minute directions for serving delicacies to my lord's own mess, but bacon and other *pièces de résistance* to the Lord Chamberlain's and Steward's messes" (K.). *Mess* also sometimes meant a set of four ; "as at great dinners the company was usually arranged into fours" (Nares). Cf. *L. L. L.* iv. 3. 207 : "you three fools lacked one fool to make up the mess," etc.

227. *Chamber-counsels.* "Private thoughts or cares" (Schmidt). The folio has "Chamber-Councels." *Counsel* and *council* are often confounded in the early eds.

228. *Cleans'd my bosom.* Cf. *Macb.* v. 3. 44 : "Cleanse the stuff'd bosom," etc.

232. *To bide upon't.* To dwell upon it, to repeat it.

234. *Hoxes.* Houghs, or hamstrings ; used by S. only here. Steevens quotes Knolles, *Hist. of the Turks :* "and with his sword hoxed his horse."

236. *Grafted in my serious trust.* Thoroughly trusted by me.

238. *Home.* "In good earnest" (Schmidt) ; or, perhaps, rather = completely, to the end. Cf. *Temp.* v. 1. 71 : "I will pay thy graces home ;" *Macb.* i. 3. 120 : "trusted home," etc.

240. *Fearful.* Full of fear ; referring to the *coward* above. See *J. C.* p. 175, note on *With fearful bravery.*

245. *Wilful-negligent.* For compound adjectives, see Gr. 2.

246. *Industriously.* Studiously, deliberately (Schmidt) ; used by S. only here.

251. *Against the non-performance.* Heath conjectures "now-performance," and explains the passage thus : "At the execution whereof such circumstances discovered themselves as made it prudent to suspend all further proceeding in it." Malone remarks that this is "a good interpretation of the original text," which he has no doubt is what S. wrote. He considers it, and we think rightly, one of those peculiar "double negatives" of which Schmidt gives many examples in his Appendix, p. 1420. See *A. Y. L.* p. 156, note on *No more do yours.* Clarke paraphrases the passage thus : "Of which the execution, when once effected, proclaimed its non-performance to have been wrong."

253. *Allow'd.* To be allowed, allowable. For *such . . . that,* see on 188 above.

256. *It's.* See on 151 above.

262. *Think.* Theo. added "it," and Hanmer gave "think 't ;" but, as Malone notes, the clause which follows—*My wife,* etc.—is the object of *think* as well as of *thought.*

266. *Hobby-horse.* The folios have "holy-horse ;" corrected by Rowe.

269. *'Shrew.* Beshrew. Cf. ii. 2. 30 below, and see *M. N. D.* p. 152.

271. *Which to reiterate,* etc. To repeat which would be a sin as great as that of which you accuse her, if the charge were true.

273. *Noses.* Omitted in Mrs. Clarke's *Concordance,* under *nose.*

275. *Note.* Mark, sign. Cf. 2 above.

278. *Noon.* The later folios have "the noon." Abbott (Gr. 484) makes the word a dissyllable. In the Var. of 1821, *blind* is put at the end of this line ; and Steevens says that *theirs, theirs* are dissyllables.

279. *The pin and web.* An early phase of cataract in the eye. Cf. *Lear,* iii. 4. 122 : "he gives the web and the pin, squints the eye," etc. Steevens, in a note on *Lear,* quotes *Every Woman in her Humour,* 1609 : "a pin and web argent, in hair du roy." Florio (as quoted by V.) defines *cataratta* as "a dimness of sight, occasioned by humours hardened in the eyes, called a cataract, or a pin and a web."

290. *Hovering.* Wavering, irresolute. Cf. *R. of L.* 1297 : "First hovering o'er the paper with her quill."

294. *Glass.* Hour-glass. Cf. *Temp.* i. 2. 240 : "At least two glasses ;" *Id.* v. 1. 223 : "but three glasses since," etc. See also iv. 1. 16 below.

295. *Her medal.* The folios have "her Medull" ("Medul" in 4th folio). Theo. gave "his medal," and the Coll. MS. has "a medal." *Like her medal* = like a medal of her. Steevens remarks that Sir Christopher Hatton is represented with a medal of Queen Elizabeth appended to his chain. Cf. *Hen. VIII.* ii. 2. 32 :

> "a loss of her
> That, like a jewel, has hung twenty years
> About his neck, yet never lost her lustre."

For *jewel*, see *T. N.* p. 154, and cf. v. 2. 32 below.

301. *Meaner form.* Lower seat, or position. See *R. and J.* p. 172. *Bench'd* = seated upon a bench, placed on a higher seat. The verb is used intransitively (= to sit on a seat of justice, to be judge) in *Lear,* iii. 6. 40 : "Bench by his side." *Rear'd to worship* = raised to honour.

304. *Galled.* The folios have "gall'd," and the later ones read "thou mightst." Steevens quotes Chapman's *Odyssey,* x. :

> "With a festival
> She 'll first receive thee ; but will spice **thy bread**
> With flowery poisons ;"

and *Id.* xviii. : "spice their pleasure's cup."

305. *A lasting wink.* Cf. *Temp.* ii. 1. 285 :

> "Whiles you, doing this,
> To the perpetual wink for aye might put
> This ancient morsel, this Sir Prudence," etc.

See also *Ham.* ii. 2. 137 : "Or given my heart a winking, mute **and** dumb."

307. *Rash.* Quick-acting. Cf. 1 *Hen. IV.* iii. 2. 61 :

> "rash bavin wits,
> Soon kindled and soon burnt ;"

2 *Hen. IV.* iv. 4. 48 : "rash gunpowder," etc.

309. *Maliciously.* "*Malignantly,* with effects *openly hurtful*" (Johnson).

310. *This crack.* Cf. *Oth.* ii. 3. 330 : "this crack of your love shall grow stronger than it was before." *Dread* = revered, held in awe.

311. *Sovereignly.* For the transposition of the adverb, see Gr. 421.

312. *I have lov'd thee.* Theo. transferred these words to the next speech, which he explained thus : "I have tendered thee well, Camillo, but I here cancel all former respect at once : if thou any longer make a question of my wife's disloyalty, go from my presence, and perdition overtake thee for thy stubbornness !" Steevens retains the old reading, and says : "Camillo is about to tell Leontes how much he had loved him. The impatience of the king interrupts him by saying, 'Make that thy question,' that is, make the love of which you boast the subject of your future conversation, and go to the grave with it." We prefer Malone's interpretation : "Make that (that is, Hermione's disloyalty, which is so

clear a point) a subject of debate or discussion, and go rot ! Dost thou
think I am such a fool as to torment myself, and to bring disgrace on me
and my children, without sufficient grounds ?"

314. *Appoint myself,* etc. We are inclined to agree with Schmidt that
this means "to dress myself," etc. Cf. "drest in an opinion" (*M. of V.* i.
1. 91), "attired in wonder " (*Much Ado,* iv. 1. 146), "wrapped in dismal
thinkings" (*A. W.* v. 3. 128), etc. Clarke thinks *appoint* may mean " point
out, mark out, stigmatize."

317. *Is goads, thorns,* etc. Abbott (Gr. 484, 509) is doubtful whether
this is a line " of four accents" or whether *goads* and *thorns* are dissyllables.

320. *Ripe.* Mature, urgent, pressing ; as in *M. of V.* i. 3. 64 : " the
ripe wants of my friend," etc.

321. *Blench.* " Fly off, be inconstant" (Schmidt). Cf. *M. for M.* iv.
5. 5 :

> "Though sometimes you do blench from this to that,
> As cause doth minister ;"

and *T. and C.* ii. 2. 68 :

> "there can be no evasion
> To blench from this, and to stand firm by honour."

322. *Fetch off.* Take off, make away with. Cf. *2 Hen. IV.* iii. 2. 324 :
" I will fetch off these justices " (that is, as Schmidt explains it, "make a
prey of them ").

325. *Sealing the injury of tongues.* Putting a stop to the mischief of
talk or scandal.

333. *I am his cup-bearer.* In Greene's tale Pandosto contriving " how
he might best put away Egistus without suspition of treacherous murder.
hee concluded at last to poyson him ; . . . and the better to bring the matter to passe he called unto him his [Egistus's] cupbearer." Franion, the
cup-bearer, endeavours to dissuade Pandosto from his purpose, but, finding it in vain, "consented as soon as opportunity would give him leave to
dispatch Egistus " (W.).

337. *Thou split'st thine own.* Thou dost rive thine own ; that is, it will
be the death of you.

345. *If I could find,* etc. Blackstone believed this to be a reference to
the death of Mary Queen of Scots ; but, as Douce remarks, the perpe-
trator of that murder *did flourish* many years afterwards. He adds : " May
it not rather be designed as a compliment to King James on his escape
from the Gowrie conspiracy, an event often brought to the people's recol-
lection during his reign, from the day on which it happened being made
a day of thanksgiving ?"

Break-neck. Halliwell quotes *An Account of the Christian Prince,*
1607 : "the very breaknecke of our ensueinge sports," etc.

357. *As he had.* As *if* he had. See Gr. 107.

360. *Wafting his eyes,* etc. Turning his eyes in the opposite direction.
For the transitive use of *falling* (=letting fall), see *J. C.* p. 169.

Mason remarks here : " This is a stroke of nature worthy of Shakespeare. Leontes had but a moment before assured Camillo that he would
seem friendly to Polixenes, according to his advice ; but on meeting him,

his jealousy gets the better of his resolution, and he finds it impossible to restrain his hatred."

365. *How! dare not!—do not?* Most editors point this "How! dare not? do not." W. has "How! dare not, do not?" The folio reads, "How, dare not? doe not?" We take the meaning to be "What! you dare not?—or is it '*do* not' that you mean? *Do* you know, and yet dare not tell me? You must mean something of the sort." The folio has an interrogation point at the end of 365, but most of the modern editors follow Capell (and Hanmer, who also changed *Do you know* to "You do know") in transferring it to the next line, as in the text. We are not sure that the change is absolutely necessary, and adopt it with some hesitation. "Do you know, and dare not?" might be an ellipsis for "Do you know, and dare not tell me?"—just as *you must* two lines below=you must *be intelligent*, you must avow it. Polixenes evidently suspects that Camillo, in saying that he dares not *know*, means that he dares not *tell* what he knows. K., V., and the Camb. editors retain the old pointing, making *Be intelligent to me* imperative.

For *intelligent*="bearing intelligence, giving information, communicative" (Schmidt), cf. *Lear*, iii. 7. 12: "Our posts shall be swift and intelligent betwixt us." See also *Id.* iii. 1. 25 and iii. 5. 12. On *thereabouts*, cf. *A. and C.* iii. 10. 29: "Ay, are you thereabouts?"

376. *Sighted like the basilisk.* With eyes like those of the fabled basilisk, that kill with a glance. See *Hen. V.* p. 183 (note on *The fatal balls*), or *R. and J.* p. 186 (note on *Death-darting eye*).

377. *Sped.* Thrived, prospered. Cf. iii. 3. 46 below: "speed thee well!" See also iv. 4. 652. For a different meaning, see *R. and J.* p. 182.

378. *Regard.* Look; as in *T. N.* ii. 5. 59, 73, etc.

379. *Thereto.* Besides. Cf. *Oth.* ii. 1. 133: "If she be black, and thereto have a wit," etc.

380. *Clerk-like.* Scholar-like. Cf. the use of *clerk*=scholar in *M. N. D.* v. 1. 93, *Hen. VIII.* ii. 2. 92, *Per.* v. prol. 5, etc.

381. *Our gentry.* Our gentle birth. Cf. *Cor.* iii. 1. 144: "gentry, title, wisdom;" *R. of L.* 569: "By knighthood, gentry, and sweet friendship's oath," etc.

382. *In whose success,* etc. To our descent from whom we owe our gentility, or nobility. For *success*=succession, cf. 2 *Hen. IV.* iv. 2. 47: "And so success of mischief shall be born," etc.

388. *Conjure.* For the accent, see *Macb.* p. 230. *Parts*=actions, tasks (Schmidt).

391. *Incidency.* Liability to fall or happen; used by S. only here. Cf. *incident*=liable to happen, in *T. of A.* v. 1. 203:

> "other incident throes
> That nature's fragile vessel doth sustain
> In life's uncertain voyage," etc.

398. *Me.* For *me*=I, cf. *A. Y. L.* i. 2. 279, i. 3. 44, *Rich. II.* iii. 3. 192, *Sonn.* 37. 14, etc. See also Gr. 210.

400. *I am appointed him.* Abbott (Gr. 220) makes *him*=by him. Clarke explains the passage thus: "I am he who is appointed," etc. The former explanation is perhaps to be preferred. The king has not been

L

mentioned in the conversation thus far, but Camillo is thinking of him.
Polixenes, who is *not* thinking of him—or at least only doubtfully—naturally asks "By *whom*, Camillo?"

404. *To vice.* To screw, move, or impel. Cf. the noun (=screw), in
Much Ado, v. 2. 21 : "you must put in the pikes with a vice." Schmidt
cites *T. N.* v. 1. 125 :

> "I partly know the instrument
> That screws me from my true place in your favour."

For verbs formed from nouns, see Gr. 290. D. reads "tice" (Heath had
suggested "'ntice"), which W. approves, though he retains *vice* in the
text. W. says that "Camillo would hardly suppose such a case as the
violent forcing of Polixenes into the arms of Hermione ;" but *vice* does
not imply any violent forcing (any more than "screws" in the passage
just quoted), but mere motive power. The meaning is that Leontes feels
as sure of it as if he had seen it, or been the agent to bring it about, like
a screw which transmits the power in a machine. Cf. *Nomenclator*, 1585 :
"A vice or gin of wood, wherewith such things as are done within out
of sight, are shewed to the beholders by the turning about of wheeles."

407. *Best.* Printed with a capital in the folio. For the allusion, cf.
Rich. II. iii. 2. 132 : "Three Judases, each one thrice worse than Judas ;"
Id. iv. 1. 170 : "So Judas did to Christ ;" 3 *Hen. VI.* v. 7. 33 : "so Judas
kiss'd his Master," etc.

412. *Swear his thought over*, etc. "Endeavour to overcome his opinion
by swearing oaths numerous as the stars" (Johnson). *Swear over*="swear
down" (*C. of E.* v. 1. 227). *Overswear*=swear again, in *T. N.* v. 1. 276.
Some editors, including W., adopt Theobald's "Swear this though over."
Lettsom suggests "Swear this oath over."

414. *Influences.* The astrological term. Cf. *Ham.* i. 1. 119, *Lear.* i. 2.
136, etc. See also Milton, *Comus*, 336 : "Or if your influence be quite
damm'd up ;" *Hymn on Nativity*, 71 : "Bending one way their precious
influence," etc.

415. *For to obey the moon.* See on 1 above. Douce compares *M. of V.*
iv. 1. 72 :

> "You may as well go stand upon the beach,
> And bid the main flood bate his usual height."

On *for to*, see *Ham.* p. 220, or Gr. 152.

417. *Whose foundation*, etc. "This folly which is erected on the foundation of settled *belief*" (Steevens).

423. *This trunk.* This body of mine. Cf. *Hen. V.* iii. 6. 163 : "this
frail and worthless trunk," etc.

425. *Whisper.* For the transitive use, cf. iv. 4. 777 : "whisper him in
your behalfs," etc.

426. *Posterns.* The smaller gates, the less frequented outlets of the
city.

429. *Discovery.* Disclosure. See *Ham.* p. 205, note on *Prevent your
discovery.*

431. *Seek to prove.* That is, by any appeal to Leontes.

433. *Thereon*, etc. And the execution of the sentence sworn by him.

436. *Thy places.* Thy honours (Steevens). Clarke sees in *places* "the

combined meaning of position as to fortune, and spot wherein to dwell; for we afterwards find that Polixenes confers manifold dignities and honours upon Camillo, and keeps him ever near to himself in Bohemia."

438. *Hence.* For the adjective use, cf. *Cymb.* iii. 2. 65 : " Our hence going " (often printed " hence-going ").

444. *Profess'd.* Professed friendship. Cf. *M. for M.* iv. 2. 192 : " by the saint whom I profess " (to whom I profess devotion), etc.

446. *Good expedition,* etc. A much disputed passage ; but on the whole Clarke's explanation seems satisfactory : " Good speed (or prosperous issue of events) befriend me, and comfort the queen ; who is, with myself, the object of his anger, but who, like myself, deserves no jot of his misconceived suspicion !" *Good expedition* may well enough be=good *speed,* or fortune (cf. iii. 2. 143 below: " the queen's speed "). If, however, we take *expedition* in its ordinary sense, we may perhaps accept Malone's paraphrase : " Good expedition befriend me by removing me from a place of danger, and comfort the innocent queen by removing the object of her husband's jealousy ; the queen, who is the subject of his conversation, but without reason the object of his suspicion !" Halliwell renders it thus : " May expedition be my friend by removing me from this scene of danger, and at the same time may my absence, the object thus accomplished, comfort the beautiful queen, who is, indeed, partly the subject of, but in no degree the reasonable object of, his suspicion." Various emendations have been proposed, none of which improve the passage. Warb. suggested " queen's " for *queen ;* " that is, be expedition my friend, and comfort the queen's !" Neither he nor Johnson could see how the *expedition* of Leontes would comfort the queen ; but, as the Camb. editors remark, " his flight without Hermione would be the best means not only of securing his own safety, but of dispelling the suspicions Leontes entertained of his queen."

Malone cites, in illustration of the phraseology, *T. N.* iii. 4. 280 : " it is something of my negligence, nothing of my purpose ;" and W. adds ii. 3. 3 below :

> " part o' the cause,
> She, the adulteress ;—for the harlot king
> Is quite beyond mine arm," etc.

450. *Avoid.* Depart, begone. Cf. *Cor.* iv. 5. 34 : " pray you, avoid." See also *Temp.* iv. 1. 142, *A. and C.* v. 2. 242, *Cymb.* i. 1. 125, etc.

Coleridge remarks on this 1st act : " Observe the easy style of chit-chat between Camillo and Archidamus as contrasted with the elevated diction on the introduction of the kings and Hermione in the second scene, and how admirably Polixenes' obstinate refusal to Leontes to stay—

> 'There is no tongue that moves ; none, none i' the world
> So soon as yours, could win me '—

prepares for the effect produced by his afterwards yielding to Hermione ; which is, nevertheless, perfectly natural from mere courtesy of sex, and the exhaustion of the will by former efforts of denial, and well calculated to set in nascent action the jealousy of Leontes. This, when once excited, is unconsciously increased by Hermione :

> 'Yet, good deed, Leontes,
> I love thee not a jar o' the clock behind
> What lady she her lord ;'

accompanied, as a good actress ought to represent it, by an **expression**
and **recoil** of apprehension that she had gone too far.

> 'At my request, he would not.'

The **first working** of the jealous fit—

> 'Too hot, too hot ;'

The **morbid tendency** of Leontes to lay hold of the merest trifles, and
his **grossness** immediately afterwards—

> 'Paddling palms and pinching fingers'—

followed by his strange loss of self-control in his dialogue with the
little boy."

ACT II.

SCENE I.—5. *As if I were a baby still.* "Can anything be more perfectly true to young boy nature? And not only in this touch, but in
the whole sketch of the child's character, S. has drawn Mamillius with
' Nature's own sweet and cunning hand ' " (Clarke).

7. *For because.* Cf. *K. John*, ii. 1. 588 : " But for because he hath not
wooed me yet," etc. On *for*=because, see Gr. 151.

11. *Taught you this.* The 1st folio has " taught 'this," which W. retains and defends. It must be admitted that in some other instances the
apostrophe seems to indicate the elision of a pronoun, etc. Cf. Gr. 461.

20. *Encounter.* Befall ; as in *Cymb.* i. 6. 112 :

> "it were fit
> That all the plagues of hell should at one time
> Encounter such revolt."

25. *A sad tale 's best for winter.* An allusion to the title of the comedy. " This first portion of the play—full of chilling suspicion, bitter injustice, and cold-blooded cruelty—harmonizes finely with the name of
The Winter's Tale ; while the warmth of youthful beauty, the glow of
young love, the return of confidence, the restoration to faith and truth,
the revival from death to life, in the latter portion of the play, poetically
consist with the ripeness of summer and the rich colouring of the season
then made its existing time " (Clarke).

33. *Was he met,* etc. Clarke says : " Admirably does the *he, his,* and
him in this line, referring to the unnamed Polixenes, serve to indicate the
perturbation of the speaker." It is possible, however, that it merely indicates the continuation of a conversation begun before the parties come
upon the stage.

37. *Censure.* Judgment, opinion. See *Ham.* p. 190 or *Macb.* p. 251.

38. *Alack, for lesser knowledge !* Oh, would that I knew less !

40. *Spider.* Henderson remarks : " That spiders were esteemed ven-
omous appears by the evidence of a person who was examined in Sir T.

Overbury's affair : 'The Countesse wished me to get the strongest poyson I could. . . . Accordingly I bought seven great spiders, and canthar-
ides.'" Malone quotes *Holland's Leaguer*, a pamphlet published in 1632 :
"like the spider, which turneth all things to poison which it tasteth."
Clarke adds, in proof that it was supposed to be necessary to see the
spider in order to be poisoned by it, the following from a play by Middleton :

> "Even when my lip touch'd the contracting cup,
> Even then to see the spider!"

For *depart* the Coll. MS. gives "apart," and St. conjectures "deep o't."
The meaning appears to be "go away unconscious of harm."

44. *Cracks his gorge.* That is, by endeavouring to vomit. Cf. *Ham.* v.
1. 207 : "my gorge rises at it ;" and see note in our ed. p. 263.

45. *Hefts.* Heavings, retchings ; used by S. only here.

50. *Discover'd.* Revealed, betrayed (not = found out). Cf. iv. 4. 701
below : "any thing that is fitting to be known, discover ;" and see on
discovery, i. 2. 429 above.

51. *Pinch'd.* Made ridiculous, served a trick (Schmidt). Cf. *T. of
S.* ii. 1. 373 : "What, have I pinch'd you, Signior Gremio?" Clarke
believes that the word is = "galled, wounded, disabled." Some make
pinch'd thing = rag-baby or puppet.

65. *Without-door.* Outward, external.

69. *Sear.* Brand ; as in *A. W.* ii. 1. 176 :

> "my maiden's name
> Sear'd otherwise," etc.

75. *Replenish'd.* Complete, consummate. Cf. *Rich. III.* iv. 3. 18: "The
most replenished sweet work of nature."

On the passage, see p. 24 above.

82. *Mannerly distinguishment.* Decent distinction.

86. *Federary.* Confederate, accomplice. S. uses the word nowhere
else, but he has *fedary* or *fœdary* in the same sense in *M. for M.* ii. 4. 122
and *Cymb.* iii. 2. 21.

One that knows, etc. "One that knows what she should be ashamed
of, even if the knowledge of it rested only in her own breast and that of
her paramour" (Malone). *But* = only ; as in 101 below. "The passage
has a confused effect (most naturally and characteristically produced, to
accord with the speaker's agitation) from *Camillo* being the antecedent
to *one that knows*, while *she 's* forms the antecedent to *and privy to this*,
etc." (Clarke).

90. *Bold'st.* Changed by Steevens to "bold," to correct the "intoler-
able roughness" of the line. The plural *vulgars* is found only here.
Hanmer gave "the vulgar." See Gr. 201, 433.

95. *Throughly.* Thoroughly. See *Ham.* p. 249.

98. *The centre.* The earth, the centre of the Ptolemaic universe. Cf.
T. and C. i. 3. 85 : "The heavens themselves, the planets, and this centre,"
etc. See also on i. 2. 138 above. Steevens quotes Milton, *Comus*, 597 :

> "if this fail,
> The pillar'd firmament is rottenness,
> And earth's base built on stubble."

100. *Is afar off guilty*, etc. Is remotely (or indirectly) guilty for only speaking. Cf. *M. W.* i. 1. 216 : "a tender, a kind of tender, made afar off by Sir Hugh here." Malone quotes *Hen. V.* i. 2. 239 :

> "Or shall we sparingly show you far off
> The Dauphin's meaning and our embassy?"

101. *Some ill planet.* For the astrological allusion, cf. i. 2. 195 above. *Aspect* (regularly accented by S. as here) was an astrological term for the peculiar position and influence of a heavenly body. Cf. *R. of L.* 14, *Sonn.* 26. 10, *T. and C.* i. 3. 92, *Lear*, ii. 2. 112, etc.

106. *But I have*, etc. Douce compares *Ham.* i. 2. 85 : "But I have that within which passeth show," etc. For *pities*, see on i. 1. 30 above, and cf. *charities* in 107 and *peaces* in 135 below.

114. *Good fools.* For *fool* as a term of pity or endearment, see *A. Y. L.* p. 151.

115. *When ye shall know*, etc. "If it be desired to know the full difference between noble pride and false pride, here is shown the former in perfection. No one better than S. knew the true distinction between them ; the right time for and due amount of self-assertion, the simplicity and severity of moral dignity : and in none of his characters are these points more notably developed than in Hermione. Her few farewell words to her mistaken husband in this speech combine in a wonderful way the essence of wifely tenderness with the utmost wifely self-respect" (Clarke). See also p. 24 above.

117. *Action.* "Charge, accusation" (Johnson) ; "law-suit" (Schmidt). Mason and Steevens make *this action I now go on* = "what I am now about to do."

123. *Be certain what you do*, etc. "In the very first words Antigonus utters, S. shows him to us in thorough contrast with Camillo. By the mere word *justice* Antigonus admits the possibility that Hermione may be guilty ; while Camillo, from first to last, feels the impossibility of her guilt. Antigonus at once proclaims himself a courtier, the man who points out to his royal master the expediency and policy of what he is about to do as touches his own person, his consort, and his heir-apparent ; Camillo is the faithful counsellor, the honest friend, the loyal servant, who strives to preserve the intrinsic honour of his king, rather than to maintain himself in his favour. Not only are these two characters finely distinguished in their delineation, the one from the other, but they are most dramatically framed for and adapted to the exigencies of the parts they are each destined to fill in the progress of the plot. Camillo, with his honourable nature and integrity of purpose, becomes the ultimate bond of reconciliation and union between the two kings and their respective children ; while Antigonus, with his courtier pliancy and lack of earnest faith—having a glimpse of the better, yet following the worse, path—becomes the agent for the king's cruelty to his infant daughter, and loses his own life in the unworthy act" (Clarke).

130. *I'll keep my stables*, etc. Malone explains the passage thus : "I'll never trust my wife out of my sight ; I'll always *go in couples* with her ; and in that respect my house shall resemble a stable, where dogs are kept in pairs." He adds that dogs are sometimes "tied up in couples

under the manger of a stable." Clarke remarks that this is "a coarse way of saying that he would not quit his wife an instant; treating her as his coach-horses and hounds are treated, which are made to go always harnessed, or leashed *in couples*." For a different interpretation, see Ingleby's *Shakespeare Hermeneutics*, p. 76 fol. Hanmer gave "stable-stand," a term of the forest-laws = a place where a deer-stealer fixes his stand to watch for the animals. The Coll. MS. has "me stable;" and the Camb. editors conjecture "my stabler" or "my stablers."

132. *Than.* The folios have "Then," which Pope and some other editors retain; but it is probably the old form for *Than*. See Gr. 70.

135. *Peaces.* See on 106 above.

137. *Abus'd.* Deceived. See *Ham.* p. 215.

Putter-on. One who *puts on* (see *Ham.* p. 257, or *Oth.* p. 180), or instigates. Cf. *Hen. VIII.* i. 2. 24:

> "they vent reproaches
> Most bitterly on you, as putter-on
> Of these exactions."

139. *Land-damn.* A stumbling-block to the commentators; probably a misprint, though no one has made a satisfactory guess at the word intended. Farmer conjectured "laudanum," Heath "half-damn," Walker "live-damn," Nicholson "Lent-damn," etc. The Coll. MS. has "lam-back" (= beat). Johnson thought *land-damn* might mean "*rid the country* of him, *condemn* him to quit the *land*." Malone suggested "land-dam" = kill, bury in earth; and Rann that *land-damn* might mean "condemned to the punishment of being built up in the earth." W. considers this last conjecture "worthy of attention as being, to say the least, not without reason," and, moreover, supported by *T. A.* v. 3. 179: "Set him breast-deep in the earth and famish him," etc. Schmidt regards it as a misprint, and proposes to read "I would—Lord, damn him!"

142. *Doing thus.* Hanmer inserts the stage-direction "*Laying hold of his arm;*" and the commentators generally agree that something of the sort is implied. Malone paraphrases the passage thus: "I see and feel *my disgrace*, as you, Antigonus, *now* feel *me*, on *my* doing thus *to you*, and *as you now* see the instruments that feel—that is, my fingers." Heath conjectured "instruments of that you feel," with "If so" for *If it be so*.

146. *Dungy earth.* The expression occurs again in *A. and C.* i. 1. 35.

152. *Forceful.* Powerful, strong; used by S. nowhere else.

155. *In skill.* Through cunning (Schmidt). Clarke explains it as "designedly, purposely."

156. *Relish.* Feel, perceive. Cf. *Temp.* v. 1. 23: "One of their kind, that relish all as sharply," etc.

158. *On 't.* Of it. Cf. ii. 2. 31, ii. 3. 15, iii. 1. 14, and iv. 4. 5 below. Gr. 182.

161. *Without more overture.* That is, without referring the matter to us, or consulting us.

166. *Approbation.* Proof, confirmation. See *Hen. V.* p. 146; and for *approve* = prove, *Ham.* p. 171.

171. *Wild.* Rash; as in iv. 4. 555 below.

In post. In haste. See *R. and J.* p. 218.

172. *Delphos.* Delphi. See on iii. 1. 2 below.

174. *Of stuff'd sufficiency.* "Of abilities more than enough" (Johnson). Cf. *Much Ado,* i. 1. 56 : "stuffed with all honourable virtues ;" and *R. and J.* iii. 5. 183 : "Stuff'd, as they say, with honourable parts." See also *Oth.* i. 3. 224 : "of most allowed sufficiency."

183. *Free.* "That is, accessible to all" (Schmidt).

SCENE II.—6. *Whom.* The 1st folio has "who" here. For *who*= whom, see Gr. 274 ; and cf. v. 1. 108 below.

11. *Access.* Accented by S. on the first syllable only in *Ham.* ii. 1. 110 (Schmidt). Cf. v. 1. 87 below.

23. *On.* In consequence of. Cf. *Rich. II.* i. 1. 9 : "If he appeal the duke on ancient malice," etc. Gr. 180.

30. *Lunes.* Lunacies, mad freaks. The word is not found elsewhere in the folio, but has been substituted by some editors for *lines* in *M. W.* iv. 2. 22 and *T. and C.* ii. 3. 139, and for *lunacies* in *Ham.* iii. 3. 7 (see our ed. p. 232). For *unsafe,* the Coll. MS. has "unsane."

33. *Honey-mouth'd.* Cf. *L. L. L.* v. 2. 334 : "honey-tongued Boyet." See also *V. and A.* 452 and *Rich. III.* iv. 1. 80.

34. *Red-look'd.* Red-looking. Cf. *Rich. II.* ii. 4. 11 : "lean-look'd prophets ;" and *M. N. D.* v. 1. 171 : "O grim-look'd night !" See also Gr. 294 and 374.

35. *Trumpet.* The word is sometimes=trumpeter or herald ; and Schmidt explains it so here. Cf. *K. John,* i. 1. 27 : "Be thou the trumpet of our wrath," etc. See also *Ham.* p. 176.

45. *Thriving.* Prosperous, successful. Cf. *J. C.* iii. 1. 13 : "I wish your enterprise may thrive," etc.

47. *Presently.* Immediately ; as very often. See *Ham.* p. 204.

49. *Hammer'd of.* Hammered on (Gr. 175), pondered. Cf. *T. G. of V.* i. 3. 18 :

> "Nor needst thou much importune me to that
> Whereon this month I have been hammering."

See also *Rich. II.* v. 5. 5 : "I 'll hammer it out."

52. *Wit.* Wisdom. See *T. N.* p. 165.

SCENE III.—2. *Weakness.* The folio reads "weaknesse, if," and is followed by some modern editors, who end the sentence at *me* in 7 below.

3. *Part o' the cause.* See on i. 2. 446 above.

4. *Harlot.* Lewd. The noun is sometimes masculine. Cf. *C. of E.* v. 1. 205 and *Cor.* iii. 2. 112 (Schmidt).

5. *The blank and level.* The mark and range, or aim. The *blank* was properly the white spot in the centre of the target. Cf. *Ham.* iv. 1. 42 : "As level as the cannon to his blank ;" *Oth.* iii. 4. 128 : "And stood within the blank of his displeasure ;" *Hen. VIII.* i. 2. 2 :

> "I stood i' the level
> Of a full-charg'd confederacy," etc.

See also iii. 2. 80 below.

6. *She.* Her. See *Oth.* p. 199, or Gr. 211.

8. *Moiety.* Portion (as in *Ham.* i. 1. 90, etc.), not a half. For the latter sense, see iii. 2. 38 and iv. 4. 790 below.

17. *Leave me solely.* Leave me to myself.

18. *Him.* That is, Polixenes, to whom his thoughts now revert.

20. *Recoil.* The plural is to be explained by the intervening *revenges.* Cf. iv. 2. 21 below : "whose loss of his most precious queen and children are even now to be afresh lamented." See also Gr. 412.

In himself too mighty, etc. Malone quotes Greene's novel : "Pandosto, although he felt that revenge was a spur to warre, and that envy always proffereth steele, yet he saw Egisthus was not only of great puissance and prowesse to withstand him, but also had many kings of his alliance to ayd him, if need should serve ; for he married the Emperor of Russia's daughter."

27. *Be second to me.* Be helpful to me, second me. Cf. the use of the noun in *Temp.* iii. 3. 103, *Cor.* i. 4. 43, etc.

30. *Free.* Free from guilt, innocent. See *Ham.* p. 213 or *A. Y. L.* p. 165.

35. *Heavings.* Deep sighs. Cf. *Ham.* iv. 1. 1 : "these sighs, these profound heaves."

37. *Medicinal.* For the accent, see *Oth.* p. 210, note on *Medicinable.*

41. *Gossips.* Sponsors at baptism. In this sense the word is both masculine and feminine. Cf. *C. of E.* v. 1. 405 : "a gossips' feast ;" *Hen. VIII.* v. 5. 13 : "My noble gossips, ye have been too prodigal," etc.

53. *Professes.* Changed by Rowe to "profess ;" but, if we may trust the collation in the Camb. ed., he does not alter *dares* below. Clarke remarks that the third person "gives the excellent effect of Paulina's speaking of another, while she thus confidently speaks of herself and her own fidelity." Both *professes* and *dares* may after all be misprints.

56. *Comforting.* Encouraging, or aiding. Cf. *T. A.* ii. 3. 209 : "Why dost not comfort me and help me out ?" *Lear,* iii. 5. 21 : "If I find him comforting the king," etc. The word properly means to strengthen (see the derivation in Wb.); and the noun is still used in a similar sense in the legal phrase "giving aid and comfort to the enemy." The Hebrew verb translated "comfort" in *Job,* ix. 27 and x. 20 is rendered "recover strength" in *Ps.* xxix. 13, and "strengtheneth" in *Amos,* v. 9. In Wiclif's version of *Isa.* xli. 7, we find "he coumfortide hym with nailes, that it shulde not be moued ;" where the A. V. has "fastened."

60. *By combat.* An allusion to the practice of "trial by combat," for a description of which see the extracts from Holinshed in *Rich. II.* p. 147 fol. and p. 159 fol.

61. *The worst.* "The *weakest,* the *least expert in the use of arms*" (Steevens).

63. *Hand.* Lay hands on. Cf. *Temp.* i. 1. 25 : "we will not hand a rope more."

67. *Mankind.* Masculine. Cf. *Cor.* iv. 2. 16 : "Are you mankind ?" Steevens quotes *The Two Angry Women of Abington,* 1599 :

> "That e'er I should be seen to strike a woman.—
> Why, she is mankind, therefore thou mayst strike her ;"

and Mason adds from one of Jonson's *Sonnets :* "Pallas, now thee I call

on, mankind maid !"   Cf. B. and F., *Monsieur Thomas :* "A plaguy
mankind girl ;" and *The Woman-Hater* : "Are women grown so mankind ?"

68. *Intelligencing.*   Carrying intelligence, acting as a go-between;
used by S. nowhere else.   Cf. *intelligencer* in 2 *Hen. IV.* iv. 2. 20 :

> "The very opener and intelligencer
>   Between the grace, the sanctities of heaven,
>   And our dull workings."

74. *Woman-tir'd.*   Hen-pecked ; the only instance of the word in S.
Tire was a term in falconry, meaning to tear and devour a prey.   Cf. *V.
and A.* *:* :

> "Even as an empty eagle, sharp by fast,
>   Tires with her beak on feathers, flesh, and bone,
>   Shaking her wings, devouring all in haste,
>   Till either gorge be stuff'd or prey be gone ;"

and *2 Hen. VI.* i. 1. 269 :

> "and like an empty eagle
>   Tire on the flesh of me and of my son."

Steevens quotes Chapman, *The Widow's Tears :* "He has given me a
bone to tire on."

78. *Forced.*   "Constrained, unnatural, false" (Schmidt); as in iv. 4. 41
below : "these forc'd thoughts," etc.   Coll. conjectures "falsed."   On
baseness, cf. *Lear,* i. 2. 10 :

> "Why brand they us
>   With base ? with baseness ? bastardy ?"

86. *Whose sting,* etc.   Cf. *Cymb.* iii. 4. 37 :

> "No, 't is slander,
>   Whose edge is sharper than the sword, whose tongue
>   Out-venoms all the worms of Nile," etc.

90. *Sound.*   The later folios have "found."

Callat.   A coarse or lewd woman.   See *Oth.* p. 201.

92. *Baits.*   Attacks, harasses.   The word literally means to set dogs
upon, as in *bear-baiting.*   Cf. *T. N.* iii. 1. 130 :

> "Have you not set mine honour at the stake
>   And bated it with all the unmuzzled thoughts
>   That tyrannous heart can think ?"

See also 2 *Hen. VI.* v. 1. 148, etc.   Here there is a play on *beat* (pronounced *bate*) and *baits.*

96. *The old proverb,* etc.   St. quotes Overbury's *Characters :* "The
devill cals him his white sonne ; he is so like him, that he is the worse
for it, and he lokes after his father."

100. *Valley.*   Apparently explained by *dimples* in apposition with it
(Schmidt).   Perhaps we should read "valleys," with Hanmer.

101. *His smiles.*   Omitted by Capell.

106. *No yellow in 't.*   For *yellow* as the colour of jealousy, cf. *M. W.* i.
3. 111 : "I will possess him with yellowness."

Suspect, as he does, etc.   This, of course, is an absurdity, but perhaps an
intentional one, as in keeping with Paulina's excited state of mind.

Clarke remarks here : "In Paulina the poet has given us a perfect picture of one of those ardent friends whose warmth of temper and want of judgment injure the cause they strive to benefit. Paulina, by her persevering iterance of the word *good*, excites Leontes' opposition, and lashes him into fury ; and now, when she has made a moving appeal in her reference to the infant's inheritance of its father's look, smile, and features, she cannot refrain from merging into reproach, ending in actual extravagance."

Cf. what Mrs. Jameson says of her : " Paulina does not fill any ostensible office near the person of the queen, but is a lady of high rank in the court — the wife of the Lord Antigonus. She is a character strongly drawn from real and common life—a clever, generous, strong-minded, warm-hearted woman, fearless in asserting the truth, firm in her sense of right, enthusiastic in all her affections ; quick in thought, resolute in word, and energetic in action ; but heedless, hot-tempered, impatient, loud, bold, voluble, and turbulent of tongue ; regardless of the feelings of those for whom she would sacrifice her life, and injuring from excess of zeal those whom she most wishes to serve. How many such are there in the world ! But Paulina, though a very termagant, is yet a poetical termagant in her way ; and the manner in which all the evil and dangerous tendencies of such a temper are placed before us, even while the individual character preserves the strongest hold upon our respect and admiration, forms an impressive lesson, as well as a natural and delightful portrait.

" In the scene, for instance, where she brings the infant before Leontes with a hope of softening him to a sense of his injustice—' an office which,' as she observes, ' becomes a woman best '—her want of self-government, her bitter, inconsiderate reproaches, only add, as we might easily suppose, to his fury. Here, while we honour her courage and her affection, we cannot help regretting her violence.

" We see, too, in Paulina, what we so often see in real life, that it is not those who are most susceptible in their own temper and feelings who are most delicate and forbearing towards the feelings of others. She does not comprehend, or will not allow for, the sensitive weakness of a mind less firmly tempered than her own. . . .

" We can only excuse Paulina by recollecting that it is a part of her purpose to keep alive in the heart of Leontes the remembrance of his queen's perfections and of his own cruel injustice. It is admirable, too, that Hermione and Paulina, while sufficiently approximated to afford all the pleasure of contrast, are never brought too nearly in contact on the scene or in the dialogue ;* for this would have been a fault in taste, and have necessarily weakened the effect of both characters. Either the serene grandeur of Hermione would have subdued and overawed the fiery spirit of Paulina, or the impetuous temper of the latter must have disturbed in some respect our impression of the calm, majestic, and somewhat melancholy beauty of Hermione."

---

* " Only in the last scene, when, with solemnity befitting the occasion. Paulina invokes the majestic figure to ' descend. and be stone no more,' and where she presents her daughter to her, ' Turn, good lady ! our Perdita is found.' "

109. *Lozel.* A worthless or cowardly fellow. Reed cites Verstegan's *Restitution,* etc., 1605 : "a Losel is one that hath lost, neglected, or cast off his owne good and welfare, and so is become lewde and carelesse of credit and honesty." S. uses the word only here. Cf. Spenser, *F. Q.* ii. 3. 4 :

> "The whyles a losell wandring by the way,
> One that to bountie never cast his mynd,
> Ne thought of honour ever did assay
> His baser brest," etc.

119. *Weak-hing'd.* "Supported by a weak hinge, ill-founded" (Schmidt). Cf. the use of *hinge* in *Oth.* iii. 3. 365 : "no hinge . . . To hang a doubt on."

127. *What needs these hands?* Referring to the persons who are putting her out of the room.

139. *Encounter with.* Cf. *V. and A.* 672 : "If thou encounter with the boar ;" 1 *Hen. IV.* i. 3. 114 : "He never did encounter with Glendower," etc.

140. *My proper.* My own. Cf. *Temp.* iii. 3. 60 : "their proper selves;" *M. for M.* v. i. 413 : "his proper tongue," etc.

143. *Fellows.* Companions, peers. See *T. N.* p. 152.

148. *Beseech you.* Rowe's emendation (perhaps unnecessary) of the "beseech'" of the folio. See on ii. 1. 11 above.

Clarke remarks here : "It is worthy of observation that the character of this speaker is delineated with so much moral beauty throughout (from that speech of chivalrous loyalty to his queen and courageous loyalty to his king, 'For her, my lord, I dare my life lay down,' etc., ii. 1. 126 fol., down to the present earnest remonstrance) that in the play of any other dramatist it would have assumed name and shape as a personage of importance , whereas, in Shakespeare's wealth of resource, and care in finishing even the most subordinate parts among his *dramatis personæ,* it merely figures as '*First Lord.*'"

150. *Dear.* Devoted, earnest, zealous. See *Temp.* p. 124 (note on *The dear'st o' th' loss*), or *Rich. II.* p. 151.

160. *Midwife.* Used contemptuously=old woman (Schmidt).

162. *This beard 's grey.* Theo. conjectured "his" for *this*, and Coll. reads "thy." Perhaps, as Malone suggests, the king takes hold of the beard of Antigonus. See on ii. 1. 142 above. *Adventure*=venture, dare ; as in i. 2. 38 above.

168. *Swear by this sword.* See *Ham.* p. 197, note on *Upon my sword;* and cf. iii. 2. 123 below.

170. *Fail.* Failure. Cf. v. 1. 27 below : "my issue's fail." See also *Hen. VIII.* i. 2. 145, *Cymb.* iii. 4. 66, etc.

172. *Lewd-tongu'd.* Vile-tongued, foul-spoken. Cf. *lewd* in *T. of S.* iv. 3. 65 : "A velvet dish ! fie, fie ! 't is lewd and filthy," etc.

178. *It own.* The reading of 1st and 2d folios ; the 3d and 4th have "its own." This old possessive *it* (or *yt*) is found fourteen times in the 1st folio, and it is curious that in seven of these it is in the combination *it own*. It is to be noted also that in the only instance in which *its* appears in our present Bible (*Lev.* xxv. 5), the ed. of 1611 has "it owne;"

and in the Geneva version of 1557 we find "it owne accorde" in *Acts,* xii. 10.   So in Sylvester's *Du Bartas,* 1605 :

> "Much like a Candle fed with it owne humour,
> By little and little it owne selfes consumer."

These and similar instances would seem to show that the old possessive *it* was often retained in this expression after it had gone out of general use ; and they justify us in assuming that *it own* is what S. probably wrote here.   *Its own* (or *it's own*), of which we have a solitary instance in i. 2. 256 above, may be the printer's variation from the MS.; though it is not improbable that the poet may have written it so.   It is evident from the number of times that *its* occurs in this play and in *Temp.*, written about the same time (seven out of the ten instances of *its* in the folio are in these two plays*), that he was getting into the way of using the new pronoun, and he might write *its own* intentionally in one passage and *it own* inadvertently or from force of habit in another.

Hudson (school ed. of *Ham.* p. 235) sneers at the editors—White, Furness, the Camb. editors, and others—who retain the possessive *it* in the text, calling this "conservatism in *it* dotage ;" but there is precisely the same reason for retaining it as for retaining any other archaic word or construction that we find in the original text.   We have no more right to change the possessive *it* to *its* than we have to change *his* to *its* in the scores of passages in which it is equivalent to the modern neuter possessive.   The "conservatism" that preserves the Elizabethan peculiarities of the poet's grammar and vocabulary is a praiseworthy characteristic of what Furnivall calls the "Victorian school" of Shakespearian criticism ; in marked contrast to the practice of the commentators of the last century, who were given to "correcting" Shakespeare's English by the standards of their own time.

182. *Commend it strangely.*   Commit it as a stranger (Johnson).

184. *Present.*   Instant, immediate ; as often.   Cf. *M. for M.* ii. 4. 152 : "Sign me a present pardon for my brother ;" *C. of E.* v. 1. 176 : "send some present help," etc.

186. *Spirit.*   Monosyllabic, as often (=*sprite*).   Gr. 463.

190. *Require.*   Nearly=deserve ; as in iii. 2. 62 below.

192. *Loss.*   Halliwell quotes Baret, *Alvearie,* 1580 : " *Losse,* hurt, properly things cast out of a shippe in time of a tempest."   Cf. *Hen. VIII.* ii. 2. 31 :

> "He counsels a divorce ; a loss of her
> That, like a jewel, has hung twenty years
> About his neck," etc.

There, as here, *loss* = casting away, discarding.

199. *'T is good speed,* etc.   Changed by Pope to "This good speed foretells," etc.   For ellipsis of nominative, see Gr. 399–402.

---

* In two of the other three (*M. for M.* i. 2. 4 and *Hen. VIII.* i. 1. 18) it is emphatic. *Hen. VIII.* is, moreover, one of the latest of the plays.   The third instance is in 2 *Hen. VI.* iii. 2. 393.

ACT III.

SCENE I.—2. *The isle.* In making "Delphos" an island, S. simply follows Greene's novel, in which the queen desires the king to send "six of his noblemen, whom he best trusted, to the isle of Delphos," etc. Perhaps, as has been suggested, Greene confounded Delphi with Delos.

4. *It caught me.* This impressed me ; *it* referring to "the whole spectacle" (Johnson).

10. *Surpris'd.* Overcame, overpowered. Cf. *V. and A.* 890 : "to surprise her heart," etc.

14. *The time is worth the use on 't.* The time we have spent is worth the trouble it has cost us (Malone) ; or, the time has been well spent.

17. *Carriage.* Conduct, management. Cf. *T. and C.* ii. 3. 140 : "The passage and whole carriage of this action," etc.

19. *Divine.* Priest. Cf. *Cor.* ii. 3. 64 : "our divines" (the Roman priests), etc.

SCENE II.—2. *Pushes,* etc. Steevens compares *Macb.* iii. 1. 117 :

> "That every minute of his being thrusts
> Against my near'st of life."

7. *Purgation.* Exculpation. See *A. Y. L.* p. 147. Here the word is a quadrisyllable. Gr. 479.

10. *Silence.* The 1st folio prints the word in italics, like a stage-direction ; the later folios have "*Silence. Enter,*" etc. Rowe made *Silence* a part of the Officer's speech, as in the text. Capell and D. assign it to a crier, and the latter compares *Hen. VIII.* ii. 4. 2. As the Camb. editors remark, there is no reason why the officer who has already spoken should not also command silence.

16. *Pretence.* Intention, design. Cf. *Macb.* ii. 3. 137 :

> "Against the undivulg'd pretence I fight
> Of treasonous malice," etc.

25. *Mine integrity,* etc. "My *virtue* being accounted *wickedness,* my assertion of it will pass but for a *lie*" (Johnson).

27. *If powers divine,* etc. Malone quotes Greene's novel : "If the *divine powers* be privie *to human actions* (*as no doubt they are*) I hope my *patience* shall make fortune *blush,* and my unspotted life shall stayne spiteful discredit."

Clarke remarks upon *as they do·* "The fervour, faith, courage, yet simplicity, summed in these three monosyllables, it would be difficult to match. Shakespeare's parentheses are often marvels of condensed power ; wonderful force and extent of meaning summed in a few words."

32. *Who.* Rowe's correction of the "Whom" of the folios.

34. *Which.* That is, which unhappiness (Malone).

36. *Take.* Captivate. Cf. *Temp.* v. 1. 313 :

> "To hear the story of your life, which must
> Take the ear strangely," etc.

37. *Owe.* Own, possess ; as very often. Cf. *A. W.* v. 3. 297, *Macb.*

i. 3. 76, i. 4. 10, iii. 4. 113, etc. We have the modern meaning in v. 1. 217 below.

38. *Moiety.* See on ii. 3. 8 above.

40. *Fore.* See *Hen. V.* p. 155.

41. *For life,* etc. "*Life* is to me now only *grief,* and as such only is considered by me ; I would therefore willingly discard it" (Johnson). Clarke paraphrases it thus : "I estimate life as I estimate grief—things that I could willingly part with, while the one I would avoid destroying, and the other I would avoid encountering."

43. *'T is a derivative,* etc. "This sentiment, which is probably borrowed from *Ecclesiasticus,* iii. 11, cannot be too often impressed on the female mind : ' The glory of a man is from the honour of his father ; and *a mother in dishonour is a reproach unto her children* ' " (Johnson).

48. *With what encounter,* etc. "With what unwarrantable familiarity of intercourse I have so far exceeded bounds, or gone astray, that I should be forced to appear thus in a public court as a criminal" (D.). For *encounter,* cf. *Much Ado,* iii. 3. 161, iv. 1. 94, *A. W.* iii. 7. 32, etc. *Uncurrent* = "objectionable" (Schmidt), unallowable (like false coin, that is not allowed to "pass"). *Strained* = twisted or wrenched aside, turned from the right course. Cf. *R. and J.* ii. 3. 19 : "Nor aught so good but, strain'd from that fair use," etc. Mason conjectured "stray'd," which he thought to be favoured by *one jot beyond the bound of honour.*

54. *Wanted less impudence,* etc. A form of "double negative" which has caused much trouble to the critics, though it is not uncommon in S. See *A. Y. L.* p. 156, note on *No more do yours.* As Johnson remarks, "according to the proper, at least according to the present, use of words, *less* should be *more,* or *wanted* should be *had.*"

57. *Due.* Appropriate, applicable.

58. *More than mistress of,* etc. Hanmer inserted "I'm" before *mistress,* but the ellipsis does not differ essentially from others in the play. The meaning evidently is, I must not acknowledge more faults than belong to me. Cf. *A. Y. L.* i. 2. 4 : "I show more mirth than I am mistress of."

62. *Requir'd.* Deserved. See on ii. 3. 190 above.

65. *As yourself commanded.* See i. 2. 174 above. "Nobly, simply, truly, does Hermione state this point of self-vindication, and with as noble a forbearance towards her most unjust husband " (Clarke).

75. *Wotting.* If they know. See Gr. 377, and cf. v. 1. 229 below : "Your honour not o'erthrown," etc. *Wot* occurs only in the present tense and participle, and this is the only instance of the latter in S.

80. *Level.* See on ii. 3. 5 above. The passage is = my life is at the mercy of your suspicions, which are like "the baseless fabric" of a dream.

81. *Which.* Referring to *life,* not to the nearer *dreams.* Cf. Gr. 218, 262, and 263.

84. *Fact.* The only meaning Schmidt gives to the word in S. is "evil deed, crime." See *Macb.* p. 225. If we take it in its simple etymological sense (from Latin *factum*), it is = deed, which is proper enough here. Johnson needlessly conjectured "pack," and Farmer "sect." "Pact"

has also been suggested. *Those of your fact* = those who do as you have done.

85. *Which to deny,* etc. "It is your *business* to deny this charge, but the mere denial will be useless—will prove nothing" (Malone).

91. *Bug.* Bugbear. See *Ham.* p. 267. For the derivation, see Wb. Cf. Ascham, *Toxophilus:* "which be the very bugges that the Psalme [*Ps.* xci. 5] meaneth on, walking in the night," etc.

92. *Commodity.* Advantage. Cf. *2 Hen. IV.* i. 2. 278: "I will turn diseases to commodity," etc.

93. *The crown and comfort of my life.* "The supreme blessing of my life" (Malone). Cf. *Cymb.* i. 6. 4: "My supreme crown of grief," etc.

98. *Starr'd most unluckily.* That is, born under "inauspicious stars" (*R. and J.* v. 3. 111). For the astrological allusion, cf. i. 2. 195, 351, and 413 above.

99. *It.* See on ii. 3. 178 above.

100. *Hal'd.* Hauled, dragged. See *Much Ado,* p. 137.

101. *Proclaim'd.* Printed "proclaimed" in the Camb. and Globe eds. The folio has "Proclaym'd."

Immodest. "Immoderate" (Schmidt); with perhaps the added idea of "indecent, unseemly," as Clarke suggests.

102. *Longs.* Belongs. See *Hen. V.* p. 160, or *Hen. VIII.* p. 162.

105. *Strength of limit.* "The limited degree of strength which it is customary for women to acquire before they are suffered to go abroad after child-bearing" (Mason). The 3d and 4th folios have "limbs" for *limit.*

108. *For life.* The folio has "no life," which might pass with Hanmer's pointing, "No! life," etc. It seems more probable, however, that "no" is a misprint. *For* is Keightley's conjecture (cf. 41 above); W. reads "my."

114. *I do refer me to the oracle.* Cf. Greene's novel: "And that this is true which I have here rehearsed, I refer myselfe to the divine oracle."

118. *The emperor of Russia,* etc. See extract from Greene, quoted on ii. 3. 20 above.

121. *Flatness.* "Downrightness, absoluteness, completeness" (Schmidt); the "flat despair" of Milton (*P. L.* ii. 143). S. uses the word only here.

122. *Pity, not revenge.* "True Shakespeare! Magnanimity and forbearance to the utmost" (Clarke).

123. *Upon this sword.* See on ii. 3. 168 above.

130. *Break up.* Cf. *M. of V.* ii. 4. 10: "to break up this" (a letter); and see note in our ed. p. 141.

131. *Hermione is chaste,* etc. Cf. Greene's novel (quoted by Malone): "*The Oracle.* Suspicion is no proofe; jealousie is an unequal judge; Bellaria is chaste; Egisthus blameless; Franion a true subject; Pandosto treacherous; his babe innocent; and the kinge shall dye without an heire, if that which is lost be not found." Coll. states that the eds. subsequent to 1588 read "the king shall *live* without an heire." It is probable, therefore, that S. used one of these later impressions.

Coleridge remarks: "Although, on the whole, this play is exquisitely respondent to its title, and even in the fault I am about to mention still a winter's tale ; yet it seems a mere indolence of the great bard not to have provided in the oracular response some ground for Hermione's seeming death and fifteen years' voluntary concealment. This might have been easily effected by some obscure sentence of the oracle ; as, for example : ' Nor shall he ever recover an heir, if he have a wife before that recovery.' " Cf. what Mrs. Jameson says, p. 25 above ; and see also the extract from Dowden, p. 32.

141. *To report it.* For reporting it. Gr. 356.

142. *Conceit.* Conception, apprehension. See *Ham.* p. 213, or *A. Y. L.* p. 162. *Speed* = fortune. Cf. the use of the verb in i. 2. 377 above.

144. [*Hermione swoons.*] "This mute succumbence to the blow dealt her in the sudden death of her little son is not only finely tragic, but profoundly true to the character of Hermione. She is not a woman 'prone to weeping,' not one who can so ease her heart of that which 'burns worse than tears drown ;' she can command her voice to utter that dignified defence of her honour, and bear the revulsion of thanksgiving at the divine intervention in her behalf with the single ejaculation of ' Praised !' but at the abrupt announcement of her boy's death she drops, without a word, stricken to the earth by the weight of her tearless woe " (Clarke).

160. *Tardied.* Retarded, delayed ; the only instance of the verb in S.

161. *Though I with death,* etc. Cf. *Macb.* i. 3. 60 :

> " Speak then to me, who neither beg nor fear
> Your favours nor your hate."

See also 203 below.

165. *Unclasp'd my practice.* Disclosed my plot. For *unclasp'd,* see *T. N.* p. 127 ; and for *practice, Ham.* p. 255 or *Much Ado,* p. 156.

166. *The hazard.* The 2d folio reads "the certain hazard," which is quite in Shakespeare's manner, though Malone calls *certain* " the most improper word that could have been chosen." Cf. *R. of L.* 1311 : " Her certain sorrow writ uncertainly ;" *Sonn.* 115. 11 : " When I was certain o'er incertainty," etc. These and similar passages may have suggested the emendation to the editor of the 2d folio. Rann conjectured "fearful hazard," and Malone "doubtful hazard."

167. *Incertainties.* S. uses this word interchangeably with *uncertainty,* as *incertain* with *uncertain.*

168. *No richer than his honour.* That is, with nothing to depend upon but his honour ; having left all his wealth behind him when he fled. St. joins this to the next sentence, putting a period after *commended.*

Glisters. Glistens (not used by S.), shines. See *M. of V.* p. 145.

169. *Thorough.* The 1st folio has " Through " (the later folios " Through my dark "), but as S. uses *thorough* and *through* interchangeably, Malone's emendation has been generally adopted. See *M. N. D.* p. 136. Cf. *throughly* in ii. 1. 95 above.

170. *Does my deeds,* etc. "This vehement retraction of Leontes, accompanied with the confession of more crimes than he was suspected of, is agreeable to our daily experience of the vicissitudes of violent tempers, and the eruptions of minds oppressed with guilt " (Johnson).

Woe the while ! Cf. *Hen. V.* iv. 7. 78 and *J. C.* i. 3. 82.

M

174. Capell inserted "rather !" after *flaying* to fill out the measure and the Coll. MS. has "burning, boiling." The folio reads "boyling?"

According to a statute of Henry VIII. persons found guilty of secret poisoning were to be boiled to death.

177. *Most worst.* For double comparatives and superlatives in S., see Gr. 11.

182. *Were but spices of it.* "Served only to season it, to give it a zest" (Schmidt). Cf. *Hen. VIII.* ii. 3. 26 : " For all this spice of your hypocrisy."

184. *Of a fool.* As a fool, in the matter of folly (Gr. 173). Johnson explains the passage : "It showed thee *first* a fool, *then* inconstant and ungrateful." Theo. changed *fool* to "soul," and Warb. *of* to "off." Coleridge says : "I think the original word is Shakespeare's. 1. My ear feels it to be Shakespearian ; 2. The involved grammar is Shakespearian : 'show thee, being a fool naturally, to have improved thy folly by inconstancy ;' 3. The alteration is most flat, and un-Shakespearian. As to the grossness of the abuse—she calls him 'gross and foolish' a few lines below."

185. *Damnable.* For the adverbial use, cf. *A. W.* iv. 3. 31 : "meant damnable," etc. Gr. 1.

186. *Thou wouldst have poison'd,* etc. "How should Paulina know this? No one had charged the king with this crime except himself, while Paulina was absent, attending on Hermione. The poet seems to have forgotten this circumstance" (Malone). Cf. p. 17 above.

191. *Shed water out of fire.* "Dropped tears from burning eyes" (Clarke). Steevens says, "shed tears of pity *o'er the damned ;*" but that would hardly be expressed by "*out of* fire."

196. *Dam.* Elsewhere applied only in contempt to a human mother. Cf. i. 2. 137 and ii. 3. 94 above.

203. *Tincture.* Colour. Cf. *T. G. of V.* iv. 4. 160 : "the lily tincture of her face ;" *Sonn.* 54. 6 : "As the perfumed tincture of the roses," etc.

207. *A thousand knees,* etc. "There is a wild exaggeration, a sublime extravagance, in Paulina's diction that poetry alone can fitly give, and which Shakespeare's poetry finely gives. These 'naked, fasting,' 'thousand *knees*'—how grandly superior, in their bold ellipse, to the 'thousand kneeling *men*' that tame correctness would have given !" (Clarke).

215. *Made fault.* Cf. *R. of L.* 804 : "all the faults which in thy reign are made ;" and *Sonn.* 35. 5 : "All men make faults," etc.

220. *What 's past help,* etc. Cf. *L. L. L.* v. 2. 28 : "past cure is still past care."

222. *Petition.* The word has been suspected, and "relation" (Sr.), "repetition" (Coll. MS.), etc., have been proposed ; but *petition* may be = appeal. Clarke remarks that Paulina has urged the king *not* to *repent,* to *betake* himself *to despair,* etc., which may justify the use of *petition.*

223. *Minded.* Reminded. Cf. *Hen. V.* iv. 3. 13 : "I do thee wrong to mind thee of it," etc.

228. *Remember thee.* Remind thee ; as in *Temp.* i. 2. 243 : "Let me remember thee what thou hast promis'd," etc.

229. *Take your patience to you.* Have patience; as in *Hen. VIII.* v. 1. 106 :

> " you must take
> Your patience to you, and be well contented
> To make your house our Tower."

SCENE III. — 1. *Perfect.* "Certain, well assured" (Johnson). Cf. *Cymb.* iii. 1. 73 :

> " I am perfect
> That the Pannonians and Dalmatians for
> Their liberties are now in arms ;"

and see *Id.* iv. 2. 118.

2. *Bohemia.* S. took his maritime Bohemia directly from Greene's novel (see. p. 17 above); but the author of *Consuelo* has attempted to save the poet's credit by showing that Ottokar II. possessed in addition to his Bohemian and other territories a *seaport* (possibly the little port of Naon) which he purchased on the Adriatic, in order to justify the boast that his dominions extended to that sea.

4. *Present.* Immediate, as in i. 2. 269, ii. 3. 184 above, and iv. 2. 46 below.

11. *Loud weather.* Cf. *Temp.* i. 1. 40 : "they are louder than the weather," etc.

20. *Some another.* That is, sometimes on the other. For the use of *another*, cf. v. 2. 71 below : "another elevated," etc. See also *M. N. D.* p. 168.

21. *A vessel of like sorrow*, etc. Cf. *J. C.* v. 5. 13 :

> " Now is that noble vessel full of grief,
> That it runs over even at his eyes."

22. *Becoming.* Comely ; referring rather to what follows than to what precedes. The Coll. MS. has "o'er-running." St. makes *becoming* = "self-restrained."

26. *The fury.* The frantic burst of grief.

32. *Weep.* The Coll. MS. gives "wend ;" but cf. 51 below : " Weep I cannot," which may refer to the injunction of the vision.

For. Because. See Gr. 151.

39. *Toys.* Explained by 1 *Hen. VI.* iv. 1. 145 : "a toy, a thing of no regard." See also *M. N. D.* p. 179.

41. *Squar'd.* Ruled. Cf. v. 1. 52 below.

45. *Earth.* Land, country ; as in *Rich. II.* ii. 1. 41, 50, iii. 2. 10, v. 1. 5, etc.

46. *Blossom.* Cf. 1 *Hen. VI.* iv. 7. 16 : "My Icarus, my blossom," etc. For *speed* = fare, see on i. 2. 377 above.

47. *Character.* "The letters of Antigonus," mentioned in v. 2. 32 below ; as *these* are the "mantle" and the "jewel," with the "gold" of 111 below.

48. *Breed.* Furnish the means of *breeding*, or bringing up.

49. *Rest.* Remain. See *A. Y. L.* p. 146. On *wretch*, cf. *R. and J.* i. 3. 44 : "The pretty wretch left crying," etc.

51. *Loss.* See on ii. 3. 192 above.

55. *Lullaby.* Cf. Greene's novel: "Shalt thou have the whistling winds for thy lullaby, and the salt sea-fome, instead of sweete milke?"

56. *Clamour.* "This clamour was the cry of the dogs and hunters; then seeing the bear, he cries *This is the chase,* or the *animal pursued*" (Johnson).

59. *Sixteen.* The early eds. have "ten," which Hanmer changed to 'thirteen;" but, as the Camb. editors remark, "if written in Arabic numerals 16 would be more likely to be mistaken for 10 than 13," and it suits the context better.

62. *Ancientry.* Old people. Cf. *Much Ado,* ii. I. 80: "full of state and ancientry;" and see note in our ed. p. 129.

63. *Boiled brains.* "Hot-headed fellows" (Schmidt). Cf. *Temp.* v. I. 60:

> "A solemn air and the best comforter
> To an unsettled fancy cure thy brains,
> Now useless, boil'd within thy skull!"

and *M. N. D.* v. I. 4: "Lovers and madmen have such seething brains."

67. *Browsing of ivy.* In Greene's novel, the shepherd goes to the sea-shore, "to see if perchance the sheepe was brouzing on the sea-ivy, whereon they doe greatly feed."

68. *A barne.* A child (Scottish *bairn*). See *Much Ado,* p. 150.

69. *A boy or a child.* According to Halliwell's *Archaic Dict.* the word *child*=girl in the Devonshire dialect; and this is confirmed by a correspondent of Knight's, who says that it is still used by the peasantry in parts of Somerset as well as Devon. W. reads "a god or a child," and quotes Greene's novel, where it is said that the shepherd, "who before had never seene so faire a babe nor so riche jewels, thought assuredly that it was *some little god,*" but when it began to cry, "knew *it was a childe.*"

70. *Scape.* See *Ham.* p. 188, or Wb. s. v.

79. *Betwixt the firmament,* etc. Cf. *Oth.* ii. I. 2:

> "it is a high-wrought flood;
> I cannot, 'twixt the heaven and the main,
> Descry a sail."

86. *Yest.* Foam; used by S. only here. Cf. *Macb.* iv. I. 53: "the yesty waves," etc.

91. *Flap-dragoned it.* Swallowed it like a *flap-dragon*—"a small combustible body [an almond, plum, or raisin] set on fire and put afloat in a glass of liquor, to be swallowed flaming" (Schmidt). See *L. L. L.* v. I. 45 and 2 *Hen. IV.* ii. 4. 267.

99. *The old man.* Changed by Theo. to "the nobleman." See p. 18 above. Malone suggests that the word *old* may have been dropped by the folio printer from the Clown's description; or, as Steevens says, the shepherd may have inferred the age of Antigonus from his inability to defend himself.

101. *Ship side.* Collier reads "ship's side;" but see *Oth.* p. 155, note on *Oath sake.*

103. *Heavy matters!* Sad business! For *look thee,* cf. *T. of A.* iv. 3. 530, etc. Gr. 212.

106. *Bearing-cloth.* "The fine mantle or cloth with which a child is usually covered when it is carried to the church to be baptized" (Percy).

108. *Changeling.* A child left by the fairies in exchange for one stolen by them. See *M. N. D.* p. 138.

110. *Made.* The folios have "mad ;" corrected by Theo. Cf. *M. N. D.* .v. 2. 18 : "we had all been made men ;" *Oth.* i. 2. 51 : "he 's made forever," etc. Farmer remarks that the word is taken from Greene's novel : "The good man desired his wife to be quiet : if she would hold peace, they were made for ever."

113. *Next.* Nearest ; as in 1 *Hen. IV.* iii. 1. 264, etc. We still speak of "the next village" (*A. Y. L.* iii. 3. 44), "the next room" (*Rich. III.* i. 4. 161), etc.

118. *Curst.* Mischievous, or savage. Cf. *V. and A.* 887 : "Finding their enemy [the boar] to be so curst ;" *Much Ado*, ii. 1. 22 : "a curst cow," etc. See also *M. N. D.* p. 167.

125. *We 'll do good deeds on 't.* "Not only does S. here record the strong feeling of reverence for the rights of sepulture among the poor, but he takes occasion to inculcate a lovely lesson of simple piety and morality—that the truest celebration of a piece of good fortune is to perform some good act in token of gratitude" (Clarke).

ACT IV.

SCENE I.—In the folios this is made the first scene of the fourth act, as here. Theo. placed it *between* the two acts as an interlude ; Warb. and Johnson put it at the end of the third act ; though the latter, who apparently did not refer to the folios, remarks that it "rather begins the fourth act than concludes the third."

W. suspects that S. did not write the speech. He says : "There could hardly be greater difference in style than that between Time's speech as Chorus and the rest of the verse in this play. The former is direct, simple, composed of the commonest words used in their commonest signification, but bald and tame, and in its versification very constrained and ungraceful ; the latter is involved, parenthetical, having a vocabulary of its own, but rich in beauties of thought and expression, and entirely untrammelled by the form in which it is written." He goes on to compare the speech with the Epilogue to *Temp.* and the Prologue to *Hen. VIII.*, which he believes to be "from the same pen, and that not Shakespeare's." All three he is inclined to ascribe to Chapman.

It seems to us that, not only the style of the speech, but its being in rhyme, may lead us to doubt whether S. wrote it. We can hardly believe it is from the same hand as the magnificent choruses in *Hen. V.*, which show how the poet could do things of that kind when he chose to do them. If he wrote this one, it must have been in some uninspired moment after the rest of the play was finished—possibly at the request of some manager who thought the gap in the action should be bridged over in that way.

6. *Sixteen years.* Steevens shows that such violations of dramatic unity were not uncommon in the plays of the time. For example, Lyly, in his *Endymion,* has an interval of forty years between two acts. Whetstone, in the dedication of his *Promos and Cassandra,* 1579, says : "The Englishman, in this quallitie, is most vaine, indiscreete, and out of order. He first grounds his worke on impossibilities : then in three houres ronnes he throwe the worlde ; marryes, gets children, makes children men, men to conquer kingdomes, murder monsters," etc.

The growth untried=the progress unconsidered, or "unattempted" (cf. Milton, *P. L.* i. 16) in the play.

8. *One self-born.* One and the same. The hyphen is in the early eds., but Schmidt objects to it as unintelligible.

14. *Glistering.* See on iii. 2. 168 above.

15. *Now seems to it.* That is, seems stale to *this present.*

17. *As.* As *if.* Gr. 107.

Leontes leaving, etc. The 1st folio prints the passage thus :

> "*Leontes* leauing
> Th' effects of his fond iealousies, so greeuing
> That he shuts vp himselfe. Imagine me
> (Gentle Spectators) that I now may be
> In faire Bohemia, and remember well,
> I mentioned a sonne o' th' Kings, which *Florizell*
> I now name to you: and with speed so pace
> To speake of *Perdita,* now growne in grace
> Equall with wond'ring."

W. and some other editors retain this pointing in the first three lines, merely changing the period after *himself* to a comma, as the later folios do. St. was the first to put the comma after *Leontes,* and make the next clause parenthetical. He is followed by the Camb. editors, D., Clarke, Delius, and others.

19. *Imagine me.* That is, with me, or for me. Cf. *L. L. L.* i. 1. 80 : "Study me how to please the eye," etc. Gr. 220.

22. *I mention'd.* The 1st folio (see above) has "mentioned ;" the later folios, "I mention here." Hanmer substituted "There is ;" and Pope, as usual, "corrected" *which* to "whom."

25. *Wondering.* Admiration. Cf. *Sonn.* 106. 14 : "Have eyes to wonder, but lack tongues to praise," etc.

26. *I list not prophesy.* I do not choose to predict. For the omission of *to,* see Gr. 349.

28. *To her adheres.* Pertains to her, concerns her.

29. *Argument.* Subject, theme. See *M. N. D.* p. 166, and cf. *Ham.* p. 207.

Of this allow=permit this (Schmidt). Malone makes *allow*=approve.

SCENE II.—4. *Fifteen.* Changed by Hanmer to "sixteen," to conform to iv. 1. 6 ; but S. is not always consistent in these matters.

5. *Been aired.* Schmidt makes this=been led forth, led about. It seems rather to be=lived, breathed the air, or been in the air—in distinction from being in the grave, which, as Polonius says (*Ham.* ii. 2. 210), "is out o' the air."

8. *O'erween.* Presume, or have the presumption. Cf. *3 Hen. VI.* iii. 2. 144 : " my heart o'erweens too much," etc.

12. *Want.* Be without, as in *M. N. D.* ii. 1. 101 : " The human mortals want their winter here," etc.

17. *Friendships.* Friendly services. Cf. *M. of V.* i. 3. 169: " I extend this friendship," etc.

22. *Are.* See on ii. 3. 20 above. Gr. 412.

25. *Approved.* Proved, as often. See *Ham.* p. 171.

28. *Missingly.* Apparently = from missing him ; that is, my missing him has led me to note his frequent absence. Steevens explains it as " at intervals," and Schmidt " with regret."

29. *Frequent to.* Addicted to, or attentive to. S. uses the adjective only here and in *Sonn.* 117. 4, where it is = conversant, intimate.

33. *Look upon his removedness.* Watch him in his absence.

36. *Is grown into an unspeakable estate.* Has become surprisingly rich.

39. *Note.* Notoriety, fame.

41. *But, I fear, the angle,* etc. But, I fear, it is the attraction, etc. The use of *but* seems at first peculiar, and Theo. substituted *and ;* but no change is absolutely required. It may be one of those cases in which the conjunction refers to something implied rather than expressed. Camillo refers to the reports of the daughter's beauty merely as an additional bit of intelligence, apparently not connecting it with Florizel's visits to the cottage ; Polixenes, perceiving this by his tone and manner, says in substance, " I, too, have heard of the pretty daughter, *but* [to *me* it isn't a fact without significance, for] I fear she is the attraction that draws my son thither." Some editors read, " but I fear the angle," etc. The folio, however, has "but (I feare) the Angle," etc.

On *angle,* see *Ham.* p. 269, and cf. the verb in i. 2. 180 above and v. 2. 79 below. Clarke suspects an allusion to Pope Gregory's pun on *Angli* and *Angeli* (see *M. of V.* p. 144, note on *Insculp'd upon*), but this is more than doubtful.

Plucks, as we have elsewhere noticed (*Ham.* p. 255 and *T. N.* p. 168), is a pet word with S.

44. *Question.* Talk, conversation. See *A. Y. L.* p. 178.

45. *Uneasy.* Difficult, *not* easy. Cf. *Temp.* i. 2. 451 :

> "but this swift business
> I must uneasy make, lest too light winning
> Make the prize light."

It is curious that the word has become obsolete in this sense, though it is still the negative of the other sense of *easy* (= comfortable). Cf. *2 Hen. IV.* iii. 1. 10: " Upon uneasy pallets stretching thee ;" and *Id.* iii. 1. 31 : " Uneasy lies the head that wears a crown." The word occurs in S. only these four times.

SCENE III.—1. *Daffodils.* Schmidt says that the poet's *daffodil* is " probably the snowdrop," but according to Ellacombe (*Plant-Lore of Shaks.*) it is the wild daffodil of England (*Narcissus pseudo-Narcissus*), the only species except *N. biflorus* which is native to the country, though many others had been introduced from other parts of Europe before the time of S.

Peer. Appear; as in iv. 4. 3 below.

2. *Doxy.* A cant word=mistress; used by S. only here. Cf. *The Roaring Girl:* "Sirrah, where 's your doxy?" Coles translates it by *meretrix.*

4. *Pale.* Paleness; with possibly a play upon the other sense=bound, limit. Cf. *V. and A.* 589: "a sudden pale . . . Usurps her cheek."

7. *Pugging.* Thievish; another cant word. In *The Roaring Girl* we find "puggards"=thieves.

11. *Aunts.* Equivalent to *doxy* above. See examples in Nares.

13. *Three-pile.* Rich velvet. It is used as a proper name in *M. for M.* iv. 3. 11: "Master Three-pile, the mercer." Steevens quotes *Ram Alley,* 1611: "With black, crimson, and tawny three-pil'd velvet."

23. *My traffic,* etc. "Autolycus means that his practice was to steal sheets and large pieces of linen, leaving the smaller pieces for the kites to build with" (Mason). These birds are said to carry off small articles of linen from the hedges where they are hung to dry, and to use them to line their nests.

25. *Under Mercury.* In the old mythology, Autolycus was a noted thief, son of Mercury, the god of thieving.

26. *With die and drab,* etc. By dicing and drabbing I was brought to "these rags" (49 below).

27. *The silly cheat.* "Petty thievery" (Schmidt); an expression taken from the slang of thieves. For *silly*=poor, petty, cf. 1 *Hen. VI.* ii. 3. 22: "a child, a silly dwarf," etc.

Gallows and knock, etc. This is in the same vein. He means that the risk of the gallows, as well as of the resistance of his victims, deters him from highway robbery

29. *I sleep out the thought of it.* "Exquisitely characteristic of this careless, merry rascal; and too true, alas! of thousands of untaught ragamuffins, whose ignorance is more their hardship than their fault" (Clarke). Coleridge remarks: "Fine as this is, and delicately characteristic of one who had lived and been reared in the best society, and had been precipitated from it by dice and drabbing, yet still it strikes against my feelings as a note out of tune, and as not coalescing with that pastoral tint which gives such a charm to this act. It is too Macbeth-like in the 'snapper-up of unconsidered trifles.'"

31. *Every 'leven wether tods.* Every eleven wethers yields a *tod,* or twenty-eight pounds of wool.

32. *Pound and odd shilling.* Twenty-one shillings. Ritson cites Stafford's *Breefe Conceipte of English Pollicye,* 1581, from which it appears that the tod of wool was then worth from twenty to twenty-two shillings. The occupation of his father (see *M. of V.* p. 9) doubtless made the poet familiar with these matters.

34. *Springe.* Snare. Cf. *Ham.* i. 3. 115: "springes to catch woodcocks." *Cock* here=woodcock, a proverbial metaphor for a simpleton. See *Ham.* p. 191.

35. *Counters.* Round pieces of metal used in reckoning. See *A. Y. L.* p. 164 ; and cf. *Oth.* p. 156, note on *Counter-caster.*

36. *Sheep-shearing feast.* The expense of these festivals was the subject of contemporary criticism. Steevens quotes *Questions of profitable and pleasant Concernings*, etc., 1594 : " If it be a sheep-shearing feast, maister Baily can entertaine you with his bill of reckonings to his maister of three shepheards wages, spent on fresh cates, besides spices and saffron pottage."

Pound. For the plural, see *Rich. II.* p. 182.

39. *Lays it on.* Cf. *Temp.* iii. 2. 160 : " he lays it on."

40. *Three-man songmen.* Singers of catches (see *T. N.* p. 136) in three parts. Halliwell, among many illustrations of the expression, cites Deloney, *Pleasant Hist. of the Gentle Craft*, 1598 : "play on the flute and beare his part in a three-mans song ;" Harrington, *Poems :*

> " When these triumvirs set that three-man's song,
> Which stablished in Rome that hellish trinity,
> That all the towne and all the world did wrong ;"

and Coryat, *Crudities*, 1611 : " That looks asquint upon a three-mans song."

41. *Means.* Tenors. Cf. *T. G. of V.* i. 2. 95 : " The mean is drown'd with your unruly base ;" and *L. L. L.* v. 2. 328 :

> " nay, he can sing
> A mean most meanly," etc.

Puritan. On contemptuous allusions to the Puritans, see *T. N.* p. 139.

43. *Warden pies.* Pies made of *wardens*, a kind of large pears. They were usually baked or roasted. Steevens quotes B. and F., *Cupid's Revenge :*

> " I would have had him roasted like a warden,
> In brown paper."

Ben Jonson puns upon the word in his *Gypsies Metamorphosed :* " A deputy tart, a church-warden pye." Halliwell adds another capital example from Strype's *Ecclesiastical Memorials :* " Quimby, a fellow of the college, was imprisoned very strictly in the steeple of New College, and half starved with cold and lack of food, and at length died. He was asked of his friends what he would eat, who said his stomach was gone for all meat, except it were a warden pie. Ye shall have it, quoth they. I would have, said he again, but two wardens baked : I mean our warden of Oxford and our warden of Winchester—London and More ; for such a warden pie might do me and the church good ; whereas other wardens of the tree can do me no good at all. Thus jesting at their tyranny through the cheerfulness of a safe conscience, he turned his face to the wall in the belfry where he lay, and after his prayers, slept sweetly in the Lord."

44. *Note* = list (Schmidt). W. explains *out of my note* as " not among the matters of which I am to take note ;" and adds : " S. would not have represented a clown in his day reading ; and manuscript, too. Had he done so, a shout of laughter, not with him but at him, would have gone up from even the penny-paying part [see *Ham.* p. 220, note on *Groundlings*] of his audience." There is something in this ; but cf. *T. N.* v. 1. 299.

45. *Race.* Root. In 1 *Hen. IV.* ii. 1. 27, we find " two razes of **ginger** ;" but it is doubtful whether *razes* is the same word.

46. *Raisins o' the sun.* That is, dried in the sun ; the only mention of raisins in S., though some see a play upon the word and *reasons* in *Much Ado*, v. 1. 211. See our ed. p. 166 ; and cf. the play on *beat* and *bait* in ii. 3. 91 above.

48. *I' the name of me.* Cf. *before me!* in *T. N.* ii. 3. 194 and *Oth.* iv. 1. 149. Theo. conjectured " name of the— ;" and some one has suggested that *me—* is an interrupted " mercy."

78. *Kills my heart.* Cf. *L. L. L.* v. 2. 149 : " Why, that contempt will kill the speaker's heart ;" *Hen. V.* ii. 1. 92 : " the king hath killed his heart," etc. In *A. Y. L.* iii. 2. 60 we have a play upon the expression.

83. *Troll-my-dames.* A corruption of the Fr. *trou-madame*, the name of a game resembling the modern *bagatelle.* It was also known as *pigeon-holes.* Farmer quotes Dr. Jones's *Buckstone Bathes* : " The ladyes, gentle woomen, wyves, maydes, if the weather be not agreeable, may have in the ende of a benche, eleven holes made, intoo the which to troule pummits, either wyolent or softe, after their own discretion : the pastyme troule in madame is termed."

88. *No more but abide.* Only make a temporary stay. *Abide* seems here to imply a transient residence, *stay* a permanent one. Cf. *Macb.* iii. 1. 140 : " I 'll call upon you straight : abide within," etc. Some make *no more but*=barely.

90. *Ape-bearer.* One who carried about a trained ape as a show.

91. *Compassed a motion.* Got possession of a puppet-show. For *compassed*, see *Hen. V.* p. 176 ; and for *motion*, cf. *T. G. of V.* ii. 1. 100 : " O excellent motion ! O exceeding puppet !" See also *Ram Alley :*

> " She 'd get more gold
> Than all the baboons, calves with two tails,
> Or motions whatsoever ;"

and *Knave in Graine*, 1640, where one of the characters asks, " Where 's the dumbe shew you promis'd me ?" and the reply is, " Even ready, my lord ; but may be called a motion ; for puppits will speak but such corrupt language you'll never understand."

95. *Prig.* Thief ; a slang word still in use.

105. *Pace softly.* Walk along slowly.

107. *Bring thee.* Accompany thee. See *Hen. V.* p. 158.

115. *Unrolled.* Struck off the roll of thieves. The Coll. MS. has " enrolled."

116. *Jog on*, etc. The lines are part of a catch in *An Antidote against Melancholy, made up in Pills compounded of witty Ballads, Jovial Songs, and merry Catches* (Reed).

117. *Hent.* Take (literally, lay hold of), clear, pass. Cf. *M. for M.* iv. 6. 14 :

> "The generous and gravest citizens
> Have hent the gates"

(that is, gone beyond or outside them). For the noun *hent*, see *Ham.* p. 234.

Scene IV.—1. *Weeds.* Garments. See *M. N. D.* p. 149.

3. *Peering.* See on iv. 3. 1 above.

5. *On't.* Cf. i. 2. 196, ii. 1. 158, etc., above.

6. *Extremes.* Johnson makes this = "the extravagance of your praises." Mason objects to this, and explains it as "the extravagance of his conduct," in dressing himself like a swain and her like a goddess. In our opinion, both are right.

It not becomes me. Cf. 401 below : "I not acquaint My father ;" and 461 : "I not purpose it." Gr. 305.

8. *The gracious mark,* etc. "The object of the nation's pride and hope" (Clarke).

9. *Wearing.* Dress ; as in *Oth.* iv. 3. 16 : "my nightly wearing."

10. *Prank'd up.* Dressed up, adorned. See *T. N.* p. 141.

11. *Mess.* See on i. 2. 217 above.

12. *With a custom.* From habit, because they are used to it.

13. *Sworn, I think,* etc. This appears to mean, as Malone explained it, that the prince, by his *swain's wearing,* seems as if he had sworn to show her a glass in which she might behold how she ought to be attired instead of being so *pranked up.* Cf. *J. C.* i. 2. 67 :

> "And since you know you cannot see yourself
> So well as by reflection, I, your glass,
> Will modestly discover to yourself
> That of yourself which you yet know not of ;"

and 2 *Hen. IV.* ii. 3. 22 :

> "he was indeed the glass
> Wherein the noble youth did dress themselves."

Malone cites this latter passage as "in *Hamlet*," from which play he *might* have quoted iii. 4. 19 :

> "You go not till I set you up a glass
> Where you may see the inmost part of you."

Theo. altered the text to

> "swoon, I think,
> To see myself i' the glass ;"

but, as Clarke remarks, *swoon* "would have an affected and exaggerated sound in the mouth of Perdita, who is composed of simplicity, rectitude, and native dignity." To our thinking, the emendation is ridiculously out of keeping with the character ; and the others that have been proposed are all as bad in their way. If a tithe of the ingenuity that has been expended in altering the early text had been devoted to its interpretation, there would be little room for emendation. In nine cases out of ten, the original reading of these much-tinkered passages affords a clearer sense than the most plausible of the revampings. We do not refer here to obvious errors in the old texts (in correcting which no editor has done more good work than Theo.), but to really difficult places, or such as at first appear so, like the present ; passages on which almost every editor has his own conjecture because no former one seems to him worth adopting—any more than *his* will seem to other editors.

17. *The difference forges dread.* The difference between your rank and mine causes me apprehension. On *forges* = frame, produce, cf. *A. W.* i. 1.

85 : " The best wishes that can be forged in your thoughts ;" *Cor.* iii. 1.
58 : " What his breast forges, that his tongue must vent," etc.

22. *Vilely bound up.* For the figure, cf. *R. and J.* i. 3. 87 : " This precious book of love, this unbound lover," etc. Johnson criticises the passage thus : " It is impossible for any man to rid his mind of his profession. The authorship of Shakespeare has supplied him with a metaphor, which, rather than he would lose it, he has put with no good propriety into the mouth of a country maid. Thinking of his own works, his mind passed naturally to the binder. I am glad that he has no hint at an editor." It strikes us that the figure might occur to any one familiar with books.

23. *Flaunts.* Finery ; the only instance of the word, or any of its derivatives, in S.

24. *Apprehend.* As Clarke notes, the word combines the idea of " fear, dread," referring to the preceding speech, with that of " conceive, entertain idea of," in connection with *jollity.*

25. *The gods themselves,* etc. Malone cites Greene's novel : " The Gods above disdaine not to love women beneath. Phœbus liked Daphne ; Jupiter Io ; and why not I then Fawnia ? One something inferior to these in birth, but far superior to them in beauty ; born to be a shepherdesse, but worthy to be a goddesse ;" and again : " The heavenly gods have sometime earthly thought ; Neptune became a ram, Apollo a shepherd : they gods, and yet in love," etc.

33. *So chaste.* The transformations of the gods were generally for illicit amours.

40. *Or I my life.* That is, or I must exchange my life for death. For *change* = exchange, cf. i. 2. 68 above. The word here is used in a double sense, like *apprehend* just above.

41. *Forc'd.* Either = false (cf. ii. 3. 78 above) or = far-fetched, out of place.

46. *Be merry, gentle.* The Coll. MS. has " girl," which Coll. adopts. He calls *gentle* " an epithet that cannot, and never did, stand alone in this way, without being followed by *maid, lady,*" etc. See, however, *A. and C.* iv. 15. 47 : " Gentle, hear me."

47. *Strangle such thoughts.* For the metaphor, cf. *T. and C.* iv. 4. 39 : " strangles our dear vows ;" *Hen. VIII.* v. 1. 157 :

> " He has strangled
> His language in his tears," etc.

50. *Nuptial.* For the use of the singular, see *M. N. D.* p. 127, or *Temp.* p. 143 ; and cf. *J. C.* p. 183, note on *His funerals.*

51. *O lady Fortune.* Cf. *Temp.* i. 2. 179 :

> " bountiful Fortune,
> Now my dear lady ;"

A. Y. L. ii. 7. 16 : " And rail'd on Lady Fortune," etc.

53. *Sprightly.* Adjectives in *-ly* are very often used as adverbs. We find " sprightly walking " in *Cor.* iv. 5. 237, where most modern eds. read " sprightly, waking."

56. *Pantler.* The servant who had charge of the pantry. Cf. *2 Hen.*

IV. ii. 4. 258 : "a' would have made a good pantler, a' would have chip-ped bread well." Cf. 342 in same scene, and see also *Cymb.* ii. 3. 129.

60. *On his shoulder, and his.* That is, leaning over to serve them.

61. *With labour,* etc. The folio points the passage thus :

> "her face o' fire
> With labour, and the thing she tooke to quench it
> She would to each one sip."

The Camb. ed. reads :

> "her face o' fire
> With labour and the thing she took to quench it,
> She would to each one sip;"

and most of the other eds. give it in essentially the same way. We fol-low W. as being more in keeping with the context. The shepherd does not mean that his wife drank so much as to increase the fire in her face ; but that even when taking a draught to cool herself she did not forget her duty to her guests.

65. *These unknown friends to us.* These friends unknown to us. See Gr. 419*a*.

74. *Rosemary and rue.* For the former, as the symbol of *remem-brance,* see *Ham.* p. 250 ; and for the latter, as the "herb of *grace*," see *Ham.* p. 251.

79. *Ancient.* Old. Cf. "ancient sir" in 350 below, and "ancientry" in iii. 3. 62 above.

82. *Carnations.* The only mention of the flower in S., though we have the *colour* in *L. L. L.* iii. 1. 146 ("a carnation ribbon") and *Hen. V.* ii. 3. 35 ("a' could never abide carnation"). For the accepted deri-vation of the name, see Wb. ; but the old spelling "coronation" ren-ders it probable that it comes from the Latin *corona,* as being a favourite flower for garlands. Pliny gives a long list of "coronamentorum gene-ra," or kinds of garland-flowers. Cf. Spenser, *Shep. Kal.* April :

> "Bring hether the Pincke and purple Cullambine,
>   With Gelliflowres ;
> Bring Coronations, and Sops in wine,
>   Worne of Paramoures :
> Strowe me the ground with Daffadowndillies,
> And Cowslips, and Kingcups, and loved Lillies :
>   The pretie Pawnce,
>   And the Chevisaunce,
> Shall match with the fayre flowre Delice."

In Lyte's *Herbal,* 1578, we also find "coronations or cornations."

Gillyvors. The folio spells it "Gilly-vors ;" and other old forms (see Wb.) are *gilover* and *gilofer.* The word is from the Fr. *giroflée,* and is not a compound of *flower.* It was only another name for the carnation, or a variety of that flower ; and "sops-in-wine" (see quotation from Spenser above) was another, from the use of the flowers for flavouring wine and beer.

86. *For.* Because ; as in iii. 3. 32 above. Douce explains Perdita's dis-like for the flower as follows : "The gillyflower or carnation is streaked, as every one knows, with white and red. In this respect it is a proper emblem of a *painted* or immodest woman ; and therefore Perdita declines

to meddle with it. She connects the gardener's *art* of varying the colours of the flowers with the art of painting the face, a fashion very prev-
alent in Shakespeare's time. This conclusion is justified by what she
says in her next speech but one."

87. *Piedness.* Variegation. Cf. *pied* in *L. L. L.* v. 2. 904 : "when daisies
pied and violets blue," etc.

89. *Mean.* For the singular, see *R. and J.* p. 189.

92. *You see, sweet maid, we marry,* etc. Shakespeare was evidently a
good gardener, and we doubt not that his grounds at New Place were as
well kept as they are now that they have been rescued from their long
desecration and made one of the most attractive spots in Stratford—
though we wish that the gardening were in the style of his time rather
than of our own.

Ellacombe remarks : " There are a great many passages scattered
throughout his works, some of them among the most beautiful that he
ever wrote, in which no particular tree, herb, or flower is mentioned by
name, but which show his intimate knowledge of plants and gardening,
and his great affection for them. It is from these passages, even more
than from those in which particular flowers are named, that we learn
how thoroughly his early country life had permanently marked his character, and how his whole spirit was most naturally coloured by it. Num-
berless allusions to flowers and their culture prove that his boyhood and
early manhood were spent in the country, and that as he passed through
the parks, fields, and lanes of his native county, or spent pleasant days
in the gardens and orchards of the manor-houses and farm-houses of the
neighbourhood, his eyes and ears were open to all the sights and sounds
of a healthy country life, and he was, perhaps unconsciously, laying up
in his memory a goodly store of pleasant pictures and homely country
talk, to be introduced in his own wonderful way in tragedies and comedies, which, while often professedly treating of very different times and
countries, have really given us some of the most faithful pictures of the
country life of the Englishman of Queen Elizabeth's time, drawn with all
the freshness and simplicity that can only come from a real love of the
subject. 'Flowers I noted,' is his own account of himself (*Sonn.* 99),
and with what love he noted them, and with what careful fidelity he wrote
of them, is shown in every play he published, and almost in every act and
every scene. His general descriptions, like his notices of particular
flowers, are never laboured, or introduced as for a purpose, but each
passage is the simple utterance of his ingrained love of the country, the
natural outcome of a keen, observant eye, joined to a great power of
faithful description and an unlimited command of the fittest language.
It is this vividness and freshness that give such a reality to all Shakespeare's notices of country life, and which make them such pleasant
reading to all lovers of plants and gardening."

For the allusion to *grafting* here, cf. *A. W.* i. 2. 54, *Hen. V.* iii. 5. 5, *Cor.*
ii. 1. 206, etc.

100. *Dibble.* An implement for piercing holes in the earth for slips or
young plants.

104. *Lavender, mints,* and *savory* are mentioned by S. only here ; *mar-*

joram (the "sweet marjoram," or *Origanum marjorana*, as is evident from the passages in *A. W.* and *Lear*) we find also in *Sonn.* 99. 7, *A. W.* iv. 5. 17, and *Lear*, iv. 6. 94.

105. *Marigold.* Not the sun-flower, as some have made it; nor the "marsh marigold" (*Caltha palustris*), which does not open and close its flowers with the sun; but probably the "garden marigold" (*Calendula officinalis*), of which Ellacombe says: "It was always a great favourite in our forefathers' gardens, and it is hard to give any reason why it should not be so in ours. Yet it has been almost completely banished, but may often be found in the gardens of cottages and old farm-houses, where it is still prized for its bright and almost everlasting flowers (looking very like a *Gazania*) and evergreen tuft of leaves, while the careful housewife still picks and carefully stores the petals of the flowers, and uses them in broths and soups, believing them to be of great efficacy, as Gerarde said they were, 'to strengthen and comfort the heart.' The two properties of the marigold—that it was always in flower, and that it turned its flowers to the sun and followed his guidance in their opening and shutting—made it a very favourite flower with the poets and emblem writers. . . . It was the 'heliotrope' or 'solsequium' or 'turnesol' of our forefathers, and is often alluded to under those names."

Of the contemporary allusions to the flower, the following from Withers is a good example:

> "When with a serious musing I behold
> The grateful and obsequious Marigold,
> How duly every morning she displays
> Her open breast when Phœbus spreads his rays;
> How she observes him in his daily walk,
> Still bending towards him her small, slender stalk;
> How when he down declines she droops and mourns,
> Bedewed, as 't were, with tears till he returns;
> And how she veils her flowers when he is gone:
> When this I meditate, methinks the flowers
> Have spirits far more generous than ours,
> And give us fair examples to despise
> The servile fawnings and idolatries
> Wherewith we court these earthly things below,
> Which merit not the service we bestow."

110. *Out, alas!* A more emphatic *alas!* Cf. *M. W.* i. 4. 37, iv. 5. 64, *R. and J.* iv. 5. 24, *Oth.* v. 2. 119, etc. So *out, alack!* in *Sonn.* 33. 11, etc.

116. *Maidenheads.* Maidenhood. See *R. and J.* p. 150.

Proserpina. Cf. *T. and C.* ii. 1. 37: "thou art as full of envy at his greatness as Cerberus is at Proserpina's beauty," etc.

118. *Dis's waggon.* Pluto's chariot. For *Dis*, cf. *Temp.* iv. 1. 89: "The means that dusky Dis my daughter got," etc.; and for *waggon*, see the description of Queen Mab's chariot in *R. and J.* i. 4. 59 fol. Cf. *A. W.* iv. 4. 34, where Helena says "Our waggon is prepar'd." Halliwell quotes Barnes, *Divils Charter*, 1607:

> "From the pale horror of eternall fire
> Am I sent with the wagon of blacke Dis."

The description of Proserpina here is taken from Ovid, *Met.* v. :

> "ut summa vestem laxavit ab ora
> Collecti flores tunicis cecidere remissis;"

thus translated by Golding:

> "And as she from the upper part her garment would have rent,
>   By chance she let her lap slip downe, and out the flowers went."

Daffodils. See on iv. 3. 1 above; and cf. the quotation from Spenser in note on 82 above, where they are called "daffadowndillies." This form of the name, now retained only in the language of children and their classic *Mother Goose,* was then common in poetry. Cf. Constable's

> "Diaphenia, like the daffadowndilly,
>   White as the sun, fair as the lily,
>   Heigh ho! how I do love thee!"

To fill out the measure, Hanmer read "early daffodils." Coleridge remarks: "An epithet is wanted here, not merely or chiefly for the metre, but for the balance, for the æsthetic logic. Perhaps *golden* was the word which would set off the *violets dim.*"

120. *Violets dim.* The violet is alluded to so often by S. that we need not refer to the passages. *Dim* is explained by Schmidt as "wanting beauty, homely;" which seems to make a stronger contrast than the poet probably intended. The meaning is not expressed by saying that the violet is homely but fragrant. It is called *dim,* we think, because it is not a brilliant or showy flower, but "half hidden from the eye" even when in full view; and we suspect that *sweeter* implies both loveliness and perfume. The reference to the *lids* of Juno's eyes has puzzled the commentators. They have even been driven to supposing that S. alluded to the Oriental practice of giving the eyelids "an obscure violet colour by means of some unguent, which was doubtless perfumed"—a sort of painting which both Perdita and he would have been disgusted at. We have no doubt that the "blue-veined violets" (*V. and A.* 125) are compared to the lids

> "white and azure lac'd
> With blue of heaven's own tinct" (*Cymb.* ii. 2. 22);

for, as we have elsewhere shown (*R. and J.* p. 172, note on *Grey eye*), the "windows" thus described, like those in *V. and A.* 482, are the *eyelids,* not the eyes. The violets, Perdita says, are lovelier than the lids of Juno's eyes and more fragrant than Cytherea's breath. For two pages of irrelevant comment on the passage, see the Var. of 1821. The critics have picked the exquisite simile to pieces, like botanists analyzing a flower, but have not got at the secret of its beauty and sweetness.

For *Cytherea,* cf. the charming "picture" in *T. of S.* ind. 2. 52:

> "Adonis painted by a running brook,
>   And Cytherea all in sedges hid,
> Which seem to move and wanton with her breath,
>   Even as the waving sedges play with wind."

See also *Cymb.* ii. 2. 14.

122. *Pale primroses.* Cf. 2 *Hen. VI.* iii. 2. 63: "Look pale as primrose, with blood-drinking sighs" (see *M. N. D.* p. 163, note on *That costs the fresh blood dear*); and *Cymb.* iv. 2. 221: "The flower that's like thy

face, pale primrose." On the next two lines, cf. Milton, *Lycidas*, 142:
"Bring the rathe primrose that forsaken dies;" and *On the Death of a Fair Infant:*

> "O fairest flower, no sooner blown but blasted,
> Soft silken Primrose fading timelessly,
> Summer's chief honour if thou hadst outlasted
> Bleak Winter's force that made thy blossoms dry."

125. *Bold oxlips.* Hanmer changed *bold* to "gold;" but Steevens says, "The *oxlip* has not a weak flexible stem like the *cowslip*, but erects itself *boldly* in the face of the sun." See *M. N. D.* p. 149, note on *Oxlips*.

126. *The crown imperial.* The *Fritillaria imperialis;* a native of the East, but early introduced from Constantinople into England, where it soon became a favourite. Chapman, in 1595, spoke of it as "Fair Crown Imperial, Emperor of flowers." Cf. Parkinson, *Paradisus Terrestris:* "The Crown Imperial for its stately beautifulnesse deserveth the first place in this our garden of delight, to be here entreated of before all other Lillies." Gerard thus describes a peculiarity of the flower: "In the bottome of each of the bells there is placed six drops of most cleere shining sweet water, in taste like sugar, resembling in shew faire Orient pearles, the which drops, if you take away, there do immediately appeare the like; notwithstanding, if they may be suffered to stand still in the floure according to his owne nature, they will never fall away, no, not if you strike the plant untill it be broken." Ellacombe adds: "There is a pretty German legend which tells how the flower was originally white and erect, and grew in its full beauty in the garden of Gethsemane, where it was often noticed and admired by our Lord; but in the night of the agony, as he passed through the garden, all the other flowers bowed their heads in sorrowful adoration, the Crown Imperial alone remaining with its head unbowed—but not for long; sorrow and shame took the place of pride, she bent her proud head, and blushes of shame and tears of sorrow soon followed, and so she has ever continued, with bent head, blushing colour, and ever-flowing tears." The legend may be found in full in *Good Words for the Young*, Aug. 1870.

127. *The flower-de-luce.* Cf. *Hen. V.* v. 2. 224: "What sayest thou, my fair flower-de-luce?" See also 1 *Hen. VI.* i. 1. 80, i. 2. 99, and 2 *Hen. VI.* v. 1. 11. It is disputed whether the poet's flower here is a lily or an iris. Ellacombe quotes St. Francis de Sales (contemporary with S.), who says: "Charity comprehends the seven gifts of the Holy Ghost, and resembles a beautiful Flower de-luce, which has six leaves whiter than snow, and in the middle the pretty little golden hammers;" a description which better fits the white lily than the iris. So Chaucer seems to connect the flower with the lily: "Her nekke was white as the Flour de Lis." On the other hand, see the quotation from Spenser in note on 82 above, where he seems to separate the lilies from the "flowre Delice." See also Bacon, *Ess.* 46: "Flower Delices, & Lillies of all Natures." In heraldry also, the fleur-de-lis and the lily are distinct bearings. The botanical writers, from Turner (1568) down to Miller (1731), also identify the flower with the iris, and with this judgment most of the recent writers agree. That S. should class it among the lilies need not trouble us, for botanical

classification was not very accurate in his day, and he does not appear to have had a scientific knowledge of the subject.

129. *Corse.* S. uses both *corse* and *corpse* (see v. 1. 58 below), though the former more frequently.

132. *Quick, and in mine arms.* For *quick* = alive, see *Hen. V.* p. 156 or *Ham.* p. 262. On the passage, cf. *Per.* v. 3. 43 :

> "O come, be buried
> A second time within these arms;"

and see *Much Ado*, p. 144, note on *Face upwards*.

134. *Whitsun pastorals.* Cf. *Hen. V.* ii. 4. 25 : "a Whitsun morris-dance." For a full account of Whitsunday sports and festivities in the olden time, see Douce's *Illustrations* or Brande's *Popular Antiquities*.

142. *Move still, still so.* "The iteration of *still* in the peculiar way that S. has used it conjoinedly with the two monosyllables *move* and *so*, gives the musical cadence, the alternate rise and fall, the to-and-fro undulation of the water—the swing of the wave—with an effect upon the ear that only a poet gifted with a fine perception would have thought of" (Clarke).

143. *Each your doing*, etc. Your manner in each act, so unparalleled in each particular, crowns the act, so that it becomes queenly. For *queens*, Sr. reads "queen's" = a queen's acts ; but the original reading carries out the bold metaphor more consistently. The *acts* are *crowned*, and themselves become *queens*.

148. *So fairly.* The 1st and 2d folios read "peepes fairely through 't," the later ones changing "peepes" to "peeps." Capell inserted the *so*, which is nearer to the origina than Hanmer's "forth." St. conjectures "through it fairly peeps," and the "Globe" ed. has "peepeth."

149. *Give you out.* Shows you ; as in *T. N.* iii. 4. 203 : "the behaviour of the young gentleman gives him out to be of good capacity," etc.

152. *Skill.* "Reason, motive ; or rather a thought caused by consideration and judgment" (Schmidt). Halliwell quotes Warner, *Albions England*, 1606 : "Our Queene deceast conceald her heire, I wot not for what skill." Clarke thinks *skill* is = design, intention. Cf. ii. 1. 155 above.

153. *To put you to 't.* See on i. 2. 16 above.

154. *Turtles.* Turtle doves ; the only meaning of the word in S. Cf. v. 3. 132 below.

156. *This is*, etc. See p. 20 above.

157. *Seems.* The Coll. MS. has "says," which W. adopts ; but no change is called for. *Nothing she does or seems* = nothing in her actions or her appearance.

160. *Makes her blood look out.* That is, makes her blush. Cf. 148 above. The folios have "look on 't ;" corrected by Theo. The Coll. MS. gives "wakes her blood ; look on 't."

Good sooth. In good sooth, in very truth. Cf. *sooth* in 336 below; and see *M. N. D.* p. 153.

162. *Garlic.* Cf. *M. N. D.* iv. 2. 43 : "And, most dear actors, eat no onions nor garlic, for we are to utter sweet breath," etc.

163. *In good time.* As Schmidt notes, equivalent to the Fr. *à la bonne heure,* and used either to denote simple assent or, as here, to express contempt or indignation. Cf. *Oth.* i. 1. 32 : " He, in good time, must his lieutenant be," etc.

168. *And boasts.* Rowe gave "and he boasts," and Capell "he boasts ;" but the ellipsis is not uncommon. See Gr. 399.

169. *But I have it,* etc. Abbott (Gr. 128) says that *but* is perhaps = "only ;" that is, " I have it *merely* on his own report, and I believe it too." " I but have it" and " I have it but" have been proposed as emendations. It seems to us, however, that with this sense of *but* it would be more natural to say "*but* I believe it." W. says : "The word here seems not to be the *but* (*be-out*)=except ; it is rather the *but* (from *botan*=to super-add) which is nearly equivalent to *and,* and of which of old was much used where we would now use that conjunction." But, as Wedgwood remarks, this distinction of Horne Tooke's between the two *buts* is " wholly untenable." It is also rejected by Prof. Mahn in Wb., and by Skeat in his new *Etymological Dict.* We may perhaps explain the *but* here by taking the words that follow as an emphatic addition to what precedes : he boasts that he has a good farm ; but as I have his word for it I believe him, for he looks truthful. Or we may say it is one of those cases in which an intermediate thought is "understood" but not expressed : he boasts of his farm ; [a mere boast, you may say] *but* I have his word for it, etc. See on iv. 2. 41 above.

A worthy feeding = a valuable pasturage. Cf. the use of *feeder* = shepherd, in *A. Y. L.* ii. 4. 99.

171. *Sooth.* Truth. See on 160 above, and cf. *M. of V.* p. 127.

175. *Who loves another.* Which loves the other. See on iii. 3. 20 above.

Featly. Dexterously, neatly. Cf. *Temp.* i. 2. 380 : " Foot it featly ;" and see note in our ed. p. 120.

180. *Not.* For the transposition, cf. 401 and 461 below. Gr. 305.

184. *Tell.* Count. See *Temp.* p. 123.

191. *Milliner.* "In the time of our author, and long afterwards, the trade of a milliner was carried on by men" (Malone). Cf. 1 *Hen. IV.* i, 3. 36 : " He was perfumed like a milliner."

193. *Dildos.* A common word in the burden of old ballads. Steevens cites one entitled *The Batchelor's Feast :* " With a hie dildo dill ;" and Malone adds from *Choice Drollery,* 1656 :

> " With a dildo, dildo, dildo,
> With a dildo, dildo, dee."

Fading (mentioned by B. J. as an Irish dance) was similarly used ; as in a song quoted by Malone : " With a fading, with a fading," etc.

194. *Stretch-mouthed.* Open-mouthed, broad-spoken.

195. *Gap.* The Coll. MS. has "jape" (=jest), which W. adopts, with the remark that the word was often spelt *gape,* though pronounced *jape.* But *gap* may be = break, or flaw. Cf. *Macb.* iii. 1. 12 and *Lear,* i. 2. 91. Puttenham, in his *Arte of Poesie,* uses the word for " parenthesis."

196. *Whoop, do me no harm, good man.* The name of an old song. In the *Hist. of Friar Bacon,* we have a ballad to the tune of " Oh ! do me no harme, good man " (Farmer).

199. *Brave.* Fine, capital. See *M. of V.* p. 154.

201. *Unbraided.* "Perhaps=not counterfeit, sterling, but probably the clown's blunder for *embroidered*" (Schmidt). Bailey, in his *Dict.*, gives *braided*=faded ; and Steevens quotes *Any Thing for a Quiet Life :* "She says that you sent ware which is not warrantable, braided ware, and that you give not London measure." *Braid* is=deceitful, in *A. W.* iv. 2. 73 : "Since Frenchmen are so braid," etc. Halliwell quotes Marston, *Scourge of Villanie*, sat. v.: "Glased his braided ware, cogs, sweares, and lies ;" and *An Iliad of Metamorphosis*, 1600 :

> "Books of this nature being once perused
> Are then cast by, and as brayed ware refused."

203. *Points.* Tagged laces, used to fasten parts of the dress, especially the breeches. See *T. N.* p. 128, note on *If one break*. Here there is a play upon the word.

204. *Inkles.* A kind of tape. Cf. *L. L. L.* iii. 1. 140 : "What 's the price of this inkle ?" and *Per.* v. prol. 8 : "Her inkle, silk, twin with the rubied cherry." The word must have been still in use in England half a century ago, as Nares and the Var. of 1821 do not explain it.

Caddises. "Worsted ribbands" (Schmidt), or what we call "galloons." Cf. 1 *Hen. IV.* ii. 4. 79 : "caddis-garter." Shirley, in his *Witty Fair One*, 1633, mentions "footmen in caddis ;" that is, having their liveries trimmed with caddis.

207. *Sleeve-hand.* Wristband, or cuff. Cotgrave defines *Poignet de la chemise* as "the sleeve-hand of a shirt." Tollet cites Leland, *Collectanea :* "A sur-coat of crimson velvet—the coller, skirts, and sleeve-hands garnished with ribbons of gold."

208. *Square.* Bosom. Cf. Fairfax, *Tasso*, xii. 64 :

> "Between her breasts the cruel weapon rives
> Her curious square, emboss'd with swelling gold."

The *square* form of the plaiting is seen in paintings of the time.

212. *You have of.* You have some of, there are some of. For the partitive *of*, cf. *A. W.* ii. 5. 50 : "I have kept of them tame," etc. See also Gr. 177.

214. *Go about.* Am going, intend. See *M. N. D.* p. 177, and cf. 683 below.

216. *Cyprus.* Crape. See *T. N.* p. 148, note on *Cypress*.

217. *Gloves,* etc. The practice of perfuming gloves is again referred to in *Much Ado,* iii. 4. 62 : "These gloves the count sent me ; they are an excellent perfume."

219. *Necklace amber,* etc. Autolycus is puffing his female wares, and says that he has some *necklace-amber*, an amber of which necklaces were made, commonly called *bead-amber*, fit to perfume a lady's chamber. Milton alludes to the perfume of amber in *S. A.* 720 : "An amber scent of odorous perfume" (T. Warton).

221. *Quoifs.* Caps, head-dresses. Cf. 2 *Hen. IV.* i. 1. 147 : "and hence, thou sickly quoif !"

223. *Poking-sticks.* These were small rods which were heated and used for adjusting the plaits of ruffs, etc. Steevens cites, among other

references to them, Middleton's *Blurt Master Constable*, 1602 : "Your ruff must stand in print, and for that purpose get poking-sticks with fair long handles, lest they scorch your hands." Stubbes, in his *Anatomie of Abuses*, describes them as "made of yron and steele, and some of brasse, kept as bright as silver, yea some of silver itselfe, and it is well if in proc-esse of time they grow not to be of gold . . . and when they come to starching and setting of their ruffes, then must this instrument be heated in the fire, the better to stiffen the ruffe," etc.

238. *Kiln-hole.* The mouth of the oven (Malone and Schmidt), or the opening for putting fuel under a stove or furnace (Steevens). Harris says that "in the Midland counties it generally means the fire-place used in making malt, and is still a noted gossiping-place."

239. *Whistle off.* The folio has "whistle of ;" and the Coll. MS. gives "whisper off." Schmidt considers *whistle* the clown's blunder for "whis-per." We do not see why it may not be his metaphorical use of the fal-coner's *whistle off* (=send off), for which see *Oth.* p. 188.

240. *Charm your tongues.* Hanmer's emendation of the "clamor your tongues" of the folios. Various other readings have been proposed, and sundry awkward attempts have been made to explain the early text. For *charm your tongues* (=check or restrain them as by a charm or spell), see *Oth.* p. 207. S. uses the phrase five times (not counting the present pas-sage), and it is common in contemporary writers.

242. *A tawdry-lace.* A rustic necklace. Cf. Spenser, *Shep. Kal.* Apr. :

> "Binde your fillets faste,
> And gird in your waste,
> For more finenesse, with a tawdrie lace ;"

and Fletcher, *Faithful Shep.* iv. 1 : "The primrose chaplet, tawdry lace, and ring." *Tawdry* is a corruption of *Saint Audrey*, or Ethelreda, on whose day (Oct. 17) a fair was held in the Isle of Ely, and probably at other places, at which gay toys of all kinds were sold. Nicholas Harps-field, in his *Hist. Eccles. Angl.*, says that St. Audrey died of a swelling in the throat, which she considered a special judgment for having been ad-dicted to wearing fine necklaces in her youth. He describes the *tawdry lace* thus : "Solent Angliae nostrae mulieres torquem quendam, ex tenui et subtili serica confectum, collo gestare ; quam Ethelredae torquem ap-pellamus, forsan in ejus quod diximus memoriam." The word *tawdry* came to be used as a noun in this sense. Cf. Drayton, *Polyolbion*, ii. :

> "Of which the Naiads and the blue Nereids make
> Them taudries for their necks ;"

and *Id.* iv. : "But with white pebbles makes her taudries for her neck."

250. *Of charge.* Of importance or value. See *R. and J.* p. 213.

252. *O' life.* "O' my life" (*M. W.* i. 1. 40), or "on my life" (v. 1. 43 below). The folio has "a life," and in many other passages it has the same corruption ; as in *R. and J.* i. 1. 1 : "A my word" (also in *T. of S.* i. 2. 108, *Cor.* i. 3. 62, etc.) ; *R. and J.* i. 3. 93 : "A plague a both the Houses," etc. So the early eds. have almost always "a clock ;" as in *Much Ado*, iii. 4. 52 (1st folio) : "fiue a clocke," etc. Halliwell explains "a life" (or "o' life") as = as my life ; and, among other examples of

the phrase, he cites *The Returne from Parnassus*, 1606 : " One that loves a-life a short sermon and a long play," etc. ; and *Ile of Gulls*, 1633 : " I love em [cherries] a-life too." This meaning might naturally enough grow out of the other, the oath coming to be used as a mere intensive.

255. *Carbonadoed.* Cut in slices and prepared for broiling. Cf. *A. W.* iv. 5. 107 : " your carbonadoed face" (that is, cut or hacked) ; and *Lear*, ii. 2. 41 : " draw, you rogue, or I 'll so carbonado your shanks." We find the noun (=steak or cutlet) in 1 *Hen. IV.* v. 3. 61 and *Cor.* iv. 5. 199.

259. *Bless me from*, etc. God preserve me from, etc. Cf. *Lear*, iii. 4. 60 : " Bless thee from whirlwinds, star-blasting, and taking !" and see *Id.* iv. 1. 60. We have the full expression in *Much Ado*, v. 1. 145 : " God bless me from a challenge !" *T. and C.* ii. 3. 32 : " heaven bless thee from a tutor," etc.

261. *Moe.* More. See *A. Y. L.* p. 176.

263. *Of a fish*, etc. In 1604 the following entry was made on the Stationers' Registers : " A strange reporte of a monstrous fish that appeared in the form of a woman, from her waist upward, seene in the sea." To this S. may allude here (Malone). Halliwell states that in the Ashmolean Museum, at Oxford, a ballad is prese ꞇꞇd with the title : " A description of a strange and miraculous fish, cast upon the sands, . . . to the tune of Bragandary." The following is a stanza from it :

> " A man on horseback, as tis try'd,
>   May stand within his mouth :
> Let none that hears it this deride,
>   For tis confirm'd for truth,
> By those who dare avouch the same ;
> Then let the writer beare no blame."

Several other of these " fish-stories" in verse have come down to our day. One of them is entitled " The discription of a rare or rather most monstrous fishe, taken on the east cost of Holland the xvij. of November, anno 1566."

275. *Passing.* Surpassingly, exceedingly. See *A. Y. L.* p. 184.

283. *Have at it.* I 'll begin it, or try it. Cf. *Cymb.* v. 5. 315 : " Have at it then" (=I 'll tell my story), etc.

301. *Sad.* Serious. See *Much Ado*, p. 121.

313. *Money 's a meddler.* That is, it has dealings with any thing. Cf. the use of *meddle*=have to do (see *T. N.* p. 152).

314. *Utter.* Cause to pass from one hand to another. See *R. and J.* p. 212.

315. *Carters.* Changed by Theo. to " goatherds," on account of the " four threes of *herdsmen*" in 325 below ; but Clarke thus shrewdly defends the old reading : " The farm-servant knows precisely what are the several callings of the rustics who personate these *men of hair*, and designates them specially ; but the king, hearing chiefly the repetition words, *shepherds, neat-herds*, and *swine-herds*, speaks of the whole twelve as ' these four threes of *herdsmen*.' "

317. *Men of hair.* That is, dressed up in goatskins, to represent *satyrs*, or what the servant blunderingly calls *saltiers*. A dance of satyrs was no unusual entertainment in that day. Froissart tells of one in which the

King of France and some of his nobles took part, and narrowly escaped being burned to death ; the hairy dress of one of the dancers taking fire from a candle, and the flames spreading to those about him.

318. *Gallimaufry.* Medley, hotchpotch. Cf. *M. W.* ii. 1. 119 : " He loves the gallimaufry" (Pistol's speech).

324. *You weary those that refresh us.* You tire these people who exert themselves for our amusement. Clarke makes *weary*=tire them "by keeping them waiting outside."

328. *Squire.* Square (Fr. *esquierre*), or foot-rule. Cf. *L. L. L.* v. 2. 474 : "Do not you know my lady's foot by the squire?" and 1 *Hen. IV.* ii. 2. 13 : "four foot by the squire."

331. *At door.* Cf. 693 below : "at palace." Gr. 90.

332. *O, father,* etc. Said in reply to something the shepherd has asked him during the dance (Mason).

334. *He 's simple, and tells much.* "These few words show that the king has been cross-questioning the old shepherd as he proposed, and with the success he then anticipated" (Clarke). Cf. iv. 2. 44 above.

337. *Handed.* Was hand in hand with, devoted myself to (Schmidt). Clarke thinks it also implies that Florizel still has Perdita by the hand (see 154 above).

338. *She.* Cf. *T. N.* i. 5. 259 : "the cruellest she alive ;" and see *A. Y. L.* p. 170. Gr. 224.

Knacks=knick-knacks ; as in *T. of S.* iv. 3. 167 : "a knack, a toy, a trick, a lady's cap," etc. See also 417 below.

341. *Marted.* Marketed, traded. Cf. *J. C.* iv. 3. 11 : "To sell and mart your offices for gold," etc.

343. *Straited.* Put into a strait ; used by S. only here.

350. *Ancient sir.* See on i. 2. 202 and iii. 3. 62 above.

351. *I take this hand,* etc. See p. 20 above.

353. *The fann'd snow,* etc. Cf. *M. N. D.* iii. 2. 141 :

> "That pure congealed white, high Taurus' snow,
> Fann'd with the eastern wind, turns to a crow
> When thou hold'st up thy hand."

356. *The hand was fair.* For the ellipsis of the relative, see Gr. 244.

372. *Take hands.* For the formal betrothal. See on i. 2. 104 above.

379. *Contract.* Often used with reference to this ceremony. See *T. N.* p. 166.

384. *Nuptial.* See on 50 above.

388. *Rheums.* Rheumatism. Cf. *M. for M.* iii. 1. 31 : "Do curse the gout, serpigo, and the rheum," etc.

389. *Dispute.* Discuss, reason upon. Cf. *Macb.* iv. 3. 220 : "Dispute it like a man," etc. *Estate*=state, condition (see *M. of V.* p. 151) ; or "interest, affairs" (Schmidt), as in *T. of A.* v. 1. 44, etc. Cf. *R. and J.* iii. 3. 63 : "Let me dispute with thee of thy estate."

395. *Reason my son,* etc. There is reason that, it is reasonable that, etc. For the ellipsis, cf. *K. John,* v. 2. 130 : "and reason too he should," etc.

401. *I not acquaint.* See on 180 above.

406. *Divorce.* Separation ; as in *C. of E.* i. 1. 105 : "this unjust divorce of us," etc.

409. *Affects.* The folio reading, changed by Pope to "affect'st ," but in verbs ending with -*t* this form of the second person appears to have been often used for euphony. See Gr. 340.

412. *Of force.* Of necessity. See *M. N. D.* p. 161. The 1st folio has "whom ;" corrected in the 2d.

413. *Cop'st with.* Meetest with, hast to do with. See *Ham.* p. 222.

415. *Fond.* Foolish (cf. iv. 1. 18 above) ; or the meanings of *silly* and *doting* may be blended, as in *M. N. D.* ii. 2. 88 and iii. 2. 114.

417. *Knack.* Plaything. See on 338 above. The folios have "shalt never see."

420. *Far.* The folios have " farre "=the Old English *ferre.* Cf. Chaucer, *C. T.* 48 : "And therto had he ridden, no man ferre ;" *Id.* 2062 : "Thus was it peinted, I can say no ferre," etc. W. prints "far'r." Cf. *near*=nearer, in *Rich. II.* iii. 2. 64, v. 1. 88 and *Macb.* ii. 3. 146. See Gr. 478. On *Deucalion,* cf. *Cor.* ii. 1. 102.

423. *Dead.* Deadly ; as in *K. John,* v. 7. 65 : "these dead news," etc.

428. *Hoop.* Pope's correction of the "hope" of the folios.

430. *Even here undone,* etc. See p. 20 above.

431. *Afeard.* Used by S. interchangeably with *afraid.* See *Macb.* p. 163.

435. *Looks on alike.* Sr. adopts Hunter's suggestion of "on all." "On both" and " on 's" have also been proposed ; but no change is necessary. It does not differ essentially from *look on*=be a looker-on, which is still good English. We say now "I stood looking on" (*T. of S.* i. 1. 155), though we have ceased to use *look upon* in the same way ; as in *T. and C.* v. 6. 10 : "He is my prize ; I will not look upon ;" 3 *Hen. VI.* ii. 3. 27 :

> "And look upon, as if the tragedy
> Were play'd in jest by counterfeiting actors," etc.

See also v. 3. 100 below. D. says that these passages are "not akin" to the present. But *look upon* as there used *implies* an object as it does here ; the only difference being that in the one case the omission of the object is the rule, while in the other it is the exception. S. takes the liberty of making the exception, as he often does in such cases.

Will 't please you, sir, be gone ? Coleridge remarks : "O how more than exquisite is this whole speech !—And that profound nature of noble pride and grief venting themselves in a momentary peevishness of resentment towards Florizel : ' Will 't please you, sir, be gone !' "

438. *Queen it.* The expression occurs again in *Hen. VIII.* ii. 3. 37. Cf. *M. for M.* iii. 2. 100 : "Lord Angelo dukes it well ;" *Cymb.* iii. 3. 85 : "to prince it," etc. Gr. 226.

441. *Nor dare to know,* etc. "By such quiet by-touches as this S. teaches morality, and not by parading lessons. Had the old shepherd had moral courage to speak out that which he knows, to declare simply that Perdita is none of his daughter, no shepherd's child, but an infant found with certain writings and rich belongings, he would have been spared the fears he here expresses. But S. not only thus instils moral precept ; he also, as a dramatist, makes his characters act characteristically, and thereby fulfils the art-necessity of protracting the final evolvement of his plot" (Clarke).

444. *To die upon the bed my father died.* That is, *upon which* my father died. Cf. *M. of V.* iv. 1. 389 : "a gift . . . of all he dies possess'd ;" *Hen. VIII.* i. 1. 196 :

> "I do pronounce him in that very shape
> He shall appear in proof," etc.

See Gr. 394.

446. *Hangman.* Executioner. See *Macb.* p. 190.

And lay me, etc. That is, bury me beneath the gallows, with no funereal service. It used to be a part of the service for the priest to throw earth upon the body.

448. *Adventure.* Venture. See on ii. 3. 162 above.

454. *Plucking back.* Pulling back. See on iv. 2. 41 above.

455. *Leash.* The cord or thong by which a hound is led. Cf. *Cor.* i. 6. 38 : "Even like a fawning greyhound in the leash," etc.

456. *Your.* The 1st folio has "my;" corrected in the 2d.

463. *How often,* etc. "The repetition of this earnest reminder to the prince of her having always striven to show him how unlikely it was that his purpose should prosper, marks the noble indignation of Perdita at the king's charge that she has sought to win Florizel, and is in strict harmony with her royal nature. It is from this imputation that she is most solicitous to free herself; it is this which most keenly wounds her ; and she remains quietly downcast, with a majesty of silent reserve worthy of Hermione's daughter" (Clarke). Cf. p. 21 above.

468. *And mar the seeds within.* Cf. *Macb.* iv. 1. 59 :

> "though the treasure
> Of nature's germens tumble all together."

471. *Fancy.* Love. See *M. N. D.* p. 129.

479. *Or the profound sea hides.* Cf. *Oth.* i. 2. 28 : "For the sea's worth ;" and see note in our ed. p. 160.

486. *Tug.* Cf. *Macb.* iii. 1. 112 :

> "And I another
> So weary with disasters, tugg'd with fortune," etc.

487. *Deliver.* Report. See *Ham.* p. 186.

488. *Whom.* The 1st folio has "who," which may be what S. wrote. Gr. 274.

489. *Opportune.* The accent is the same as in *Temp.* iv. 4. 511, the only other instance of the word in S. Gr. 490. For *our* the folios have "her ;" corrected by Theo.

490. *Rides.* For the omission of the relative, cf. 356 above. Gr. 244.

494. *Easier for advice.* More inclined to take advice.

495. *Hark, Perdita.* "Here is a perfect, though apparently slight, example of Shakespeare's dramatic art. By Florizel's taking Perdita apart we are made to perceive how he sees that she stands silently—as it were irresponsively and unassentingly by—while he speaks to Camillo ; and how he hastens to confer with her, and convince her of his unswerved faith, and persuade her to his views : moreover, it affords opportunity for Camillo's soliloquy, which tells the audience his plan " (Clarke).

499. *Do him love.* Cf. *R. and J.* iii. 3. 118 : " doing damned hate upon thyself ;" *R. of L.* 597 : "do him shame," etc. Gr. 303.

503. *Fraught.* Charged, burdened. See *T. N.* p. 162.

Curious = requiring care, embarrassing. Cf. *T. and C.* iii. 2. 70:
"What too curious dreg espies my sweet lady in the fountain of our
love?"

509. *As thought on.* As thought of, as they are estimated.

513. *Ponderous.* Weighty; that is, having weight or force with you.
Cf. *Lear*, i. 1. 80:

> "my love's
> More ponderous ["richer" in quartos] than my tongue."

519. *Forefend.* Forbid. See *Oth.* p. 206.

521. *Your discontenting father*, etc. Strive to pacify your angry father
and bring him round to approving the match. On *qualify*, cf. *K. John*,
v. 1. 13, *T. and C.* ii. 2. 118, etc. *Discontenting* (=discontented) occurs
nowhere else in S. See Gr. 372.

527. *The unthought-on accident.* The unexpected discovery made by
Polixenes. *On* = *of*, occurs very often in this play. For *to* after *guilty*,
cf. *C. of E.* iii. 2. 168: "But lest myself be guilty to self-wrong," etc.
Guilty to = responsible for.

528. *So we profess*, etc. "As *chance* has driven me to these extremities,
so I commit myself to *chance*, to be conducted through them" (Johnson).

532. *Undergo.* Undertake; as in ii. 3. 164 above. Cf. *T. G. of V.* v.
4. 42:

> "What dangerous action, stood it next to death,
> Would I not undergo for one calm look!"

2 Hen. IV. i. 3. 54: "How able such a work to undergo," etc.

538. *Asks.* An ellipsis of the nominative (Gr. 399), with a change of
construction (cf. Gr. 415).

540. *Fresh.* Cf. 411 above. As Clarke remarks, the epithet "serves
to set her in her clear-complexioned, clear-souled purity and brightness
before us, with the bloom of a country maiden's cheek, and the white tem-
ples of the born princess."

541. *Unkindness.* See *T. N.* p. 156, note on *Unkind.* *Kindness*
seems to combine the ideas of good-will and tenderness (see *Much Ado*,
p. 118).

544. *Colour for my visitation.* Pretext for my visit. Cf. *Hen. VIII.*
i. 1. 178:

> "Under pretence to see the queen his aunt—
> For 't was indeed his colour," etc.

See also on i. 1. 6 above.

546. *Comforts.* Consolations. Cf. *A. and C.* v. 1. 62:

> "give her what comforts
> The quality of her passion shall require," etc.

549. *Betwixt us three.* The only instance of this inaccurate use of *betwixt* that we have noticed in S.

550. *Point you forth.* Point out the way before you. Cf. *Cymb.* v. 5.
454:

> "and thy lopp'd branches point
> Thy two sons forth."

Sitting. Audience or interview. Theo. changed the word to "fitting."

551. *That.* *So* that; as in i. 1. 27 and in 146 above. Gr. 283.

552. *Have your father's bosom.* Are intrusted with his inmost thoughts or feelings. Cf. *M. for M.* iv. 3. 139 : "And you shall have your bosom on this wretch " (that is, your heart's desire), etc.

554. *Sap.* Life, promise. Cf. *A. and C.* iii. 13. 192 : "There 's sap in 't yet."

558. *But as you shake off one,* etc. Cf. *Cymb.* i. 5. 54 :

> " To shift his being
> Is to exchange one misery with another."

559. *Who.* Often used for *which,* especially in personifications. Gr. 264.

566. *Take in.* Take, conquer. Cf. *Cor.* i. 2. 24 : "To take in many towns " (see also iii. 2. 59) ; *A. and C.* i. 1. 23 : "Take in that kingdom, and enfranchise that " (see also iii. 7. 24 and iii. 13. 83) ; *Cymb* IV. 2. 121 :

> " Who call'd me traitor, mountaineer, and swore
> With his own single hand he 'd take us in," etc.

On the passage, see p. 21 above.

570. *I' the rear o' our birth.* The folios have " i' th' reare ' our Birth " (" rear " in 4th folio). W. reads " i' th' rear 'f our birth."

572. *Sir ; for this,* etc. The folio reads :

> " Your pardon Sir, for this,
> Ile blush you Thanks."

Some editors point it thus :

> " Your pardon, sir, for this;
> I 'll blush you thanks."

576. *Medicine.* Physician. Cf. *A. W.* ii. 1. 75 :

> " I have seen a medicine
> That 's able to breathe life into a stone," etc.

See also *Macb.* p. 248.

577. *Furnish'd.* Equipped, fitted out (like *appointed* in 581 below); as in *T. G. of V.* ii. 7. 85 : "To furnish me upon my longing journey," etc.

578. *Appear.* That is, appear *so,* or *like Bohemia's son.* Rowe prints " appear in Sicily—;" and the Coll. MS. has " appear't."

587. *Pomander.* " A little ball made of perfumes, and worn in the pocket, or about the neck, to prevent infection in times of plague " (Grey). It was also worn for the sake of the perfume or as a mere ornament. Halliwell devotes several pages to it, with illustrations showing its varied form and construction. Steevens quotes the following recipe for the article from *Lingua, or a Combat for the Tongue,* 1607 : " Your only way to make a good Pomander is this : Take an ounce of the purest garden mould, cleansed and steeped seven days in change of motherless rosewater. Then take the best labdanum, benjoin, both storaxes, amber-gris and civet and musk. Incorporate them together, and work them into

what form you please. This, if your breath be not too valiant, will make
you smell as sweet as my lady's dog."   Various other recipes are given
in books of the time.   Cf. Drayton, *Quest of Cynthia* ·

> " As when she from the water came,
> Where first she touch'd the mould,
> In balls the people made the same,
> For pomander, and sold ;"

and *Polyolbion*, iv. :

> " Her moss most sweet and rare,
> Against infectious damps for pomander to wear."

A book of devotion, published in 1578, was entitled " A Pomander of
Prayers."

For *table-book*, see *Ham.* p. 197, note on *Tables*.

589. *Hallowed.* "This alludes to beads often sold by Romanists,
as made particularly efficacious by the touch of some relic " (Johnson).

591. *Was best in picture.* Had the best look.

594. *Pettitoes.* Literally, pig's feet ; here used contemptuously.

596. *In ears.* Mason conjectured " in their ears."

598. *Nothing.* Perhaps, as Clarke suggests, there is a pun on *nothing*
and *noting*. See *Much Ado*, p. 136.

600. *Whoo-bub.* Hubbub, outcry ; used by S. only here.

602. *Choughs.* For this bird, see *Macb.* p. 221 or *Temp.* p. 127.

604. *Nay, but my letters*, etc. A reply to something said by Florizel
during their conversation apart. Cf. 332 above.

608. *Who.* Whom ; as in v. 1. 109 below, etc. Gr. 274.

617. *Discase.* Undress; as in *Temp.* v. 1. 85 : " I will discase me." So
uncase in *L. L. L.* v. 2. 707 and *T. of S.* i. 1. 212.

620. *Some boot.* Something to boot. Cf. *T. and C.* iv. 5. 40 : " I 'll
give you boot," etc. The modern phrase occurs in *Sonn.* 135. 2, *T. and C.*
i. 2. 260, *Macb.* iv. 3. 37, etc.

624. *Flayed.* Jocosely = stripped ; perhaps playing on *discase*, the word
case being often = skin (Clarke). There may be a play on *case* in 792 below.

628. *Earnest.* Used quibblingly, referring to his question just before,
and to the *earnest* he had received. Cf. *T. G. of V.* ii. 1. 162 :

> " *Speed.* But did you perceive her earnest?
> " *Valentine.* She gave me none, except an angry word."

See also *C. of E.* ii. 2. 23 :

> " *Antipholus of Syracuse.* Think'st thou I jest? Hold, take thou that, and that.
>   [*Beating him.*
> " *Dromio of Syracuse.* Hold, sir, for God's sake ! now your jest is earnest ;
> Upon what bargain do you give it me?"

635. *Disliken*, etc. Disguise your natural appearance.

637. *Over.* Elliptical for " over us," if the text is right. Rowe added
" you," and the Coll. MS. gives " ever." Schmidt would point the passage thus :

> " that you may
> (For I do fear eyes) over to shipboard," etc.

638. *I see the play so lies*, etc. "The reluctance shown by Perdita to join in the scheme of proposed flight, disguise, and consequent deception thereby entailed, is delineated with a force none the less remarkable from the extreme delicacy of the depicting, and which serves strikingly to characterize this transparent-natured creature " (Clarke).

642. *What have we*, etc. Apparently a mere dramatic expedient to allow the introduction of Camillo's soliloquy.

647. *To force. As* to force. For the ellipsis, see Gr. 281.

648. *Review.* See again. S. uses the verb only here and in *Sonn.* 74. 5.

663. *I would not do 't.* Hanmer transposed the *not*, placing it after *were ;* and Capell put it after *thought.* Autolycus means that it would not be honesty to tell the king, but a sort of knavery—that is, it would be playing a mean trick on those who had paid him well—and he decides on the greater knavery of concealing the plot.

666. *Hot.* Ardent, active. Cf. *L. L. L.* ii. 1. 120: "Your wit 's too hot, it speeds too fast, 't will tire."

667. *A careful man.* Clarke calls attention to the exquisite wit and humour of this expression in the mouth of Autolycus.

670. *Changeling.* See on iii. 3. 108 above. "Most true to Shakespeare's philosophy of ' good in every thing ' is the making this lout of a shepherd-clown have just the spark of sense to perceive that in their present strait honesty is the best policy " (Clarke).

683. *To go about.* To be going, to attempt. See on 214 above.

687. *I know how much.* Hanmer inserted " not " after *know ;* but the blunder was probably intentional.

690. *Fardel.* Bundle ; spelt " Farthell " in the folio. It is used half a dozen times in this play, but elsewhere only in *Ham.* iii. 1. 76.

693. *At palace.* The folio prints " at ' Pallace." The apostrophe may be a misprint, or it may indicate the omission or absorption of *the.* Cf. Gr. 90.

696. *Excrement.* Beard. The word is applied to the hair or beard in five out of the six passages in which S. uses it. See *Ham.* p. 238.

698. *An it like.* If it please. Cf. *Ham.* ii. 2. 80 : " It likes us well ;" and see note in our ed. p. 202.

701. *Having.* Estate, property. See *A. Y. L.* p. 178.

702. *Discover.* Disclose, tell me. See on ii. 1. 50 above.

706. *But we pay them for it*, etc. Daniel has suggested " *not* with stamped coin, but stabbing steel," comparing *Oth.* iii. 4. 5 : " He 's a soldier ; and for one to say a *soldier lies* is *stabbing.*" Autolycus appears to have mystified the critic here, as he doubtless did the clown. When he said that *tradesmen* " often give us soldiers the lie," he probably meant that they do it by lying about their wares (a trick that he was sufficiently familiar with) ; but, he adds, " we pay them for it with stamped coin, not with stabbing steel "—as they deserve, or as you would suppose. *Tradesmen* could hardly be said to be in the habit of giving *soldiers* the lie in the literal sense of the phrase.

709. *Had like.* See *A. Y. L.* p. 197, note on *And like.*

710. *Taken yourself with the manner.* A legal phrase = taken yourself in the fact. Cf. *L. L. L.* i. 1. 206 : "The manner of it is, I was taken with the manner ;" and 1 *Hen. IV.* ii. 4. 347 : "O villain, thou stolest a cup of sack eighteen years ago, and wert taken with the manner, and ever since thou hast blushed extempore."

714. *Measure.* "Stately tread" (Malone). Cf. *measure*=a grave dance ; as in *Much Ado*, ii. 1. 80, etc.

716. *For that.* Because. Cf. ii. 1. 7 above. *Insinuate*="intermeddle" (Schmidt) ; as in *Rich. III.* i. 4. 152 : "he would insinuate with thee," etc.

717. *Or touze.* The 1st folio has "at toaze," the later folios "or toaze." The word is probably the same that we have in *M. for M.* v. 1. 313 :

> "to the rack with him! we 'll touze you
> Joint by joint."

There it means to pull apart ; here it is apparently=draw out.

718. *Cap-a-pe.* From head to foot. See *Ham.* p. 186.

724. *A pheasant.* "As he was a suitor from the country, the clown supposes his father should have brought a present of *game*, and therefore imagines, when Autolycus asks him what *advocate* he has, that by the word *advocate* he means a *pheasant*" (Steevens). Reed says : "In the time of Queen Elizabeth there were Justices of the Peace called *Basket Justices*, who would do nothing without a present ; yet, as a member of the House of Commons expressed himself, 'for half a dozen of *chickens* would dispense with a whole dozen of penal statutes.'" Halliwell gives this apt illustration from the *Journal* of the Rev. Giles Moore, 1665 : "I gave to Mr. Cripps, solicitor, for acting for me in obtaining my qualification, and effecting it, £1 10s., and I allowed my brother Luxford for going to London thereupon, and presenting my lord with two brase of pheasants, 10s.," etc. The patron to whom he sent the game was "Charles, Lord Goring, Earle of Norwich."

Some editors needlessly change *pheasant* to "present."

731. *He wears them not handsomely.* A "touch of nature." The shepherd, though a simple man, has an instinctive perception of the difference between a true gentleman and a vulgar fellow disguised as one.

734. *By the picking on 's teeth.* Johnson remarks : "It seems that to pick the teeth was at this time a mark of some pretension to greatness or elegance. So the Bastard, in *King John* [i. 1. 190], speaking of the traveller, says : 'He and his toothpick at my worship's mess.'" See also *A. W.* i. 1. 171 : "just like the brooch and the toothpick, which wear not now ;" and *Id.* iii. 2. 8 : "Why, he will . . . pick his teeth and sing."

738. *Such . . . which.* See on i. 1. 22 above.

750. *In hand-fast.* "In custody ; properly in *mainprise*, in the custody of a friend on security given for appearance" (D). In *Cymb.* i. 5. 78, *hand-fast*=betrothal, marriage-engagement.

754. *Wit.* Inventive power ; as in *V. and A.* 472, *M. for M.* v. 1. 368, *L. L. L.* i. 2. 191, etc.

755. *Germane.* Akin, related. Cf. *T. of A.* iv. 3. 344 : "germane to the lion," etc.

758. *Sheep-whistling.* Whistling for sheep, tending sheep.

759. *Come into grace.* That is, "undergo such ample grace and honour" (*M. for M.* i. 1. 24) as to marry the prince.

766. *'Nointed over with honey,* etc. Reed cites a book which S. may have seen, *The Stage of Popish Toyes,* 1581 : "he caused a cage of yron to be made, and set it in the sunne : and, after annointing the pore Prince over with hony, forced him naked to enter in it, where hee long time endured the greatest languor and torment in the worlde, with swarmes of flies that dayly fed on him ; and in this sorte, with paine and famine, ended his miserable life."

769. *The hottest day,* etc. "That is, the hottest day foretold in the almanac" (Johnson). Malone quotes the title of a Calendar of the time : "An Almanack and Prognostication made for the year of our Lord God 1595."

773. *Traitorly.* Traitorous ; used by S. only here.

775. *Being something gently considered.* If I have a gentlemanlike consideration given me (Steevens) ; a delicate hint at a bribe. Cf. *The Ile of Gulls,* 1633 : "Thou shalt be well considered, there's twenty crowns in earnest."

777. *Tender.* Present, introduce.

781. *And though.* Some editors read "an though." Cf. Gr. 101.

790. *Moiety.* See on ii. 3. 8 above.

792. *Case.* See on 624 above.

813. *Back.* The Coll. MS. has "luck."

814. *Aboard him.* Aboard his ship. Cf. v. 2. 110 below : "aboard the prince."

815. *Shore.* The only instance of the verb in S. Cf. Gr. 290.

ACT V.

Scene I.—2. *Make.* See on iii. 2. 215 above.

6. *Whilst I remember,* etc. See p. 32 above.

12. *True, too true,* etc. In the folios, the first *true* is joined to the preceding speech ; corrected by Theo. See p. 23 above.

14. *Or from the all,* etc. Cf. *Temp.* iii. 1. 47 :

> "but you, O you,
> So perfect and so peerless, are created
> Of every creature's best!"

See also *A. Y. L.* iii. 2. 149–160.

19. *Good now.* For this "vocative use" of *good,* see *Ham.* p. 173.

27. *Fail.* See on ii. 3. 170 above.

29. *Incertain.* See on iii. 2. 167 above.

30. *Well.* At rest. Cf. *A. and C.* ii. 5. 33 : "We use to say, the dead are well." See also *R. and J.* p. 208. As Henley remarks, this use of *well* seems to have been suggested by 2 *Kings,* iv. 26.

31. *Repair.* Restoration. Cf. *Sonn.* 3. 3, *K. John,* iii. 4. 113, etc.

35. *Respecting.* Considering, if we consider. Cf. 2 *Hen. VI.* iii. 1. 24 : "Respecting what a rancorous mind he bears," etc.

42. *As my Antigonus*, etc.   For the construction, see Gr. 354, and cf. 416.

45. *Contrary.*   Schmidt puts this among the cases in which the accent is on the penult (like *K. John*, iv. 2. 198, *Ham.* iii. 2. 221, etc.), but the other accent, which is the more common one in S., suits the verse quite as well, if not better.   See *Ham.* p. 227.

46. *Oppose against.*   Cf. *T. of A.* iii. 4. 80, *Lear*, ii. 4. 179, iv. 7. 32, *Rich. II.* iii. 3. 18, etc.

52. *Squar'd.*   See on iii. 3. 41 above.

57–60. *Would make*, etc.   The 1st folio prints the passage thus :

> " would make her Sainted Spirit
> Againe possesse her Corps, and on this Stage
> (Where we offendors now appeare) Soule-vext,
> And begin, why to me?"

Various emendations have been proposed ; as " (Where we offend her now) appear soul-vex'd " (Theo.) ; " (Were we offenders now) appear " (Heath) ; " (Where we offend her) now appear " (Spedding) ; " Where we 're offenders now, appear " (anon. in Camb. ed.), etc.   The reading in the text is that of K., St., W., the Camb. ed., and others.   Of course *are* is understoood with *offenders*.   The reading " we're " is very plausible, but the ellipsis is not unlike many others in this play.

In 60, Capell's reading " Begin, ' And why to me?' " is adopted by many editors.   There is probably some corruption in the original.   Malone explains *why to me ?* as = " why to me did you prefer one less worthy?" and Boswell (better, we think) "why such treatment to me?"

61. *Cause.*   The 1st and 2d folios have " such cause."

Incense.   Incite, instigate.   See *Much Ado*, p. 166.

65. *That.*   So that.   Cf. i. 1. 27 and iv. 4. 146 above.

66. *Rift.*   Burst, split.   S. uses the verb only here and in *Temp.* v. 1. 45 : "and rifted Jove's stout oak."   Elsewhere he has *rive ;* as in *Cor.* v. 3. 153 : "That should but rive an oak," etc.

75. *Affront.*   Come before, meet.   Cf. *Ham.* iii. 1. 31 :

> "That he, as 't were by accident, may here
> Affront Ophelia," etc.

See *Ham.* p. 216.

I have done.   In the folios, these words are at the end of the preceding speech ; the emendation is Capell's, and is generally adopted. K. and Halliwell retain the old reading.

80. *Walk'd your first queen's ghost.*   That is, *if* it walked ; the inversion being like that still common with *have*, *be*, etc.   Cf. 107 below.

83. *In breath.*   Elsewhere used only in the modern sense ; as in *T. and C.* v. 7. 3 : " Strike not a stroke, but keep yourselves in breath," etc.

85. *Gives out.*   Cf. iv. 4. 149 above.

87. *Access.*   Accented regularly on the last syllable, except in *Ham.* ii. 1. 110.

90. *Out of circumstance.*   Without ceremony.   See *Much Ado*, p. 145 and *Ham.* p. 197.

91. *Visitation.*   See on i. 1. 6 above.   *Fram'd* = planned, premeditated.

94. *Piece of earth.* Cf. iv. 4. 32, 411 above.

97. *Grave.* Changed in the Coll. MS. to "**grace.**" Clarke thus defends the old reading : " It affords befitting antecedent to *colder than that theme ;* and it has fine poetic propriety in itself, as embodying the collective beauties of the supposed dead queen in her *grave,* and impressing upon Paulina's hearers the point of which she wishes them to be convinced—that Hermione's remains repose in the *grave.*" To us the antithesis of *thy grave*—thou in thy grave—and *what's seen now*—the living beauty before our eyes—seems very forcible. A good actress would make an impressive " point " of it.

102. *Shrewdly.* Combining the ideas of *much* and *badly.* Cf. *Hen. V.* p. 170.

109. *Who.* See on iv. 4. 608 above.

113. *With.* By. Cf. v. 2. 60 below : " with a bear." **Gr.** 193.

114. *Embracement.* Used by S. oftener than *embrace.* Cf. *C. of E.* i. 1. 44, *Rich. III.* ii. 1. 30, etc.

117. *Full a.* The 3d and 4th folios have " a full."

124. *Unfurnish.* Deprive. Cf. *T. A.* ii. 3. 56 : " Unfurnish'd of er well-beseeming troop."

126. *Print,* etc. Cf. ii. 3. 98 above.

139. *On him.* Changed by Steevens to " upon ;" but cf. *Temp.* iii. 2. 53 : " whom Destiny . . . Hath caus'd to belch up you." For other examples, see Gr. 249.

141. *At friend.* On terms of friendship ; the reading of the 1st folio, changed to " as friend " in the 2d. See Gr. 143 ; and cf. *to friend* in *A. W.* v. 3. 182, *J. C.* iii. 1. 143, etc.

142. *But.* But *that.* Cf. *Temp.* i. 2. 414 : " And but he 's something stain'd," etc. **Gr.** 120.

143. *Waits upon worn times.* Attends old age. *Seiz'd* = fallen upon, attacked.

155. *Adventure.* Hazard, risk ; as in *C. of E.* ii. 2. 218 : " at all adventures," etc. Cf. the use of the verb in *Temp.* ii. 1. 187, *M. of V.* i. 1. 143, etc. See also i. 2. 38, ii. 3. 162, and iv. 4. 448 above.

156. *Libya.* Douce conjectured " Lydia " or " Lycia."

169. *Climate.* Try the climate, sojourn ; the only instance of the verb in S.

Holy. Good, blameless. Cf. *Temp.* v. 1. 62 : " Holy Gonzalo, honourable man," etc. *Graceful* in next line = full of grace, gracious.

181. *Attach.* Arrest ; a law term. See *R. and J.* p. 217 or *Rich. II.* p. 186.

188. *Whiles.* See Gr. 137.

196. *In question.* Under examination ; not simply " in conversation " (cf. iv. 2. 44 above), as some explain it.

201. *O my poor father !* On the silence of Perdita up to this point, see p. 21 above.

203. *Our contract celebrated.* Our betrothal consummated by marriage. See *T. N.* p. 160 (note on *Plight me,* etc.) and p. 166 (note on *Contracted*).

206. *The odds for high and low,* etc. The chances for the high and

O

the low in rank are equally uncertain. Douce sees here a quibble on the false dice called *high and low ;* as in *M. W.* i. 3. 95.

213. *Worth.* Johnson remarks : " *Worth* signifies any kind of *worthiness,* and among others that of high descent. The king means that he is sorry the prince's choice is not in other respects as worthy of him as in beauty." For *worth*=wealth, fortune, see *T. N.* p. 151.

215. *Visible an enemy.* Appearing visibly as an enemy.

218. *Remember since,* etc. Remember when, etc. ; that is, recollect when you were no older than I am. *Since* is used in this way only after verbs of remembering. Cf. *M. N. D.* ii. 1. 149 :

> " Thou rememberest
> Since once I sat upon a promontory," etc.

See Gr. 132.

219. *With thought of such affections.* Thinking of such feelings as you then had. recalling what your feelings then were.

223. *Sir, my liege.* A form of address used also in *Temp.* v. 1. 245 and *Cymb.* iii. 1. 16. Cf. *Sir, my lord,* in i. 2. 306 above, and *sir, my gracious lord,* in iv. 4. 5.

229. *Your honour,* etc. If your honour, etc. Cf. iii. 2. 75 above. Gr. 377.

SCENE II.—4. *Deliver.* Relate. Cf. iv. 4. 487 above and 25 below.

5. *Amazedness.* Cf. *M. W.* iv. 4. 55 : " We two in great amazedness will fly."

6. *Only this,* etc. The folio prints the passage thus : " onely this (me thought) I heard the Shepheard say, he found the child." Some eds. give it : " only this, methought I heard the shepherd say he found the child."

17. *Importance.* Import (Malone and Schmidt).

18. *Of the one.* That is, of the one or the other.

19. *Happily.* Haply ; as often. See *T. N.* p. 158 or *Ham.* pp. 175, 208. Gr. 42.

23. *Ballad-makers.* These writers were in the habit of turning any extraordinary event to account. Cf. the subjects of the ballads that Autolycus has for sale (iv. 4. 254 fol. above), and see note on iv. 4. 263.

29. *Pregnant by circumstance.* Made plausible by the circumstances or the facts in the case. *Pregnant* is elsewhere used in a similar sense =about to appear as truth, highly probable. Cf. *M. for M.* ii. 1. 23, *Oth.* ii. 1. 239, *A. and C.* ii. 1. 45, and *Cymb.* iv. 2. 235.

32. *Jewel.* Used for any personal ornament of gold or precious stones. See on i. 2. 295 above.

33. *Character.* Handwriting. Cf. *Ham.* iv. 7. 53 : " 'T is Hamlet's character," etc.

35. *Affection.* Disposition ; as in *Macb.* iv. 3. 77 : " my most ill-compos'd affection," etc. *Affection of nobleness*=innate nobility.

46. *Favour.* Look, aspect. See *Ham.* p. 263 or *M. N. D.* p. 130.

51. *Clipping.* Embracing. Cf. *K. John.* v. 2. 34 : " Neptune's arms, who clippeth thee about." See also *Oth.* p. 192.

52. *Weather-bitten.* Changed to " weather-beaten " in the 3d folio.

Henley remarks : " *Conduits* representing a human figure were here-
tofore not uncommon. One of this kind, a female form, and weather-
beaten, still exists at Hoddesdon in Herts." Cf. *R. and J.* iii. 5. 129 :
" How now ! a conduit, girl ? what, still in tears ?" and see note in our
ed. p. 196.

55. *To do it.* That is, to *describe* it. Hanmer changed *do* to "draw,"
and the Coll. MS. has "show." Sr. conjectures "do it justice."
Malone compares *Temp.* iv. 1. 10 :

> " For thou shalt find she will outstrip all praise,
> And make it halt behind her."

66. *Wracked.* For the spelling, see *T. N.* p. 162.

71. *Another.* The other. Cf. iii. 3. 20 and iv. 4. 176 above.

79. *Angled.* See on iv. 2. 41 above. On the passage, see p. 22
above.

85. *Who was most marble.* Even those who were of the hardest natures, or least susceptible of emotion ; not "most petrified with wonder,"
as Steevens explained it.

92. *Julio Romano.* He was born in 1492 and died in 1546. For the
anachronism, see pp. 13, 17, and 35 above. *Eternity*=immortality ; as
in *R. of L.* 214 : " Or sells eternity to get a toy," etc.

93. *Of her custom.* " That is, *of her trade*—would draw her customers
from her " (Johnson).

94. *Is he her ape.* Does he ape her. Cf. *Cymb.* ii. 2. 31 : " O sleep,
thou ape of death !"

101. *Removed.* Remote, retired. See *A. Y. L.* p. 177.

102. *Piece.* Add to, increase.

106. *Unthrifty to our knowledge.* " Not intent on increasing, and hence
not increasing, our knowledge " (Schmidt).

116. *Relished.* Schmidt makes *relish* here=" have a pleasing taste."
The meaning may be, it would have counted as nothing in comparison
with my discredits, would not have served to give them even a "relish
of salvation " (*Ham.* iii. 3. 92).

120. *Moe.* See on i. 2. 8 above.

122. *Denied.* Refused. See *R. and J.* p. 159.

123. *See you these clothes ?* See p. 36 above.

139. *Preposterous.* The clown's blunder for *prosperous* (Schmidt).

144. *For we must be gentle,* etc. The shepherd's expression of " No-
blesse oblige." See on iii. 3. 125 above.

152. *Franklins.* Freeholders, yeomen ; above *villains* or serfs, but not
gentlemen (Johnson). Cf. *Cymb.* iii. 2. 79 :

> " A riding-suit, no costlier than would fit
> A franklin's housewife."

156. *A tall fellow of thy hands.* " An active, able-bodied man, who
will stand the test " (Schmidt). Cf. *M. W.* i. 4. 27 : " he is as tall a man
of his hands as any is between this and his head ; he hath fought with a
warrener." Cf. *T. N.* p. 123, note on *Tall.* Halliwell cites Cotgrave,
Fr. Dict. : " *Haut à la main, Homme à la main, Homme de main,*—A
man of his hands ; a man of execution or valour ; a striker, like enough

to lay about him ;" and Palsgrave, *Lesclaircissement*, etc., 1530: "I*r*e is a tall man of his handes, *C'est ung habille homme de ses mains.*"

160. *To my power.* To the best of my ability.

164. *Picture.* That is, painted statue.

165. *Masters.* Patrons. Cf. *L. L. L.* iv. 1. 106: "From my Lord Biron, a good master of mine." Whalley cites a letter from Fisher, Bishop of Rochester, when in prison, to Cromwell: "Furthermore, I beseeche you to be gode master unto one in my necessities," etc.

SCENE III.—**4.** *Home.* In full. See on i. 2. 238 above, and cf. *Ham.* p. 232, note on *Tax him home.*

11. *Content.* Satisfaction, pleasure. See *Oth.* p. 174.

12. *Singularities.* Rarities, curiosities. Cf. *singular* in iv. 4. 144 above.

18. *Lonely.* The 1st folio has "Louely," the later folios "Lovely;" corrected by Hanmer. Warb. defended "lovely," explaining it as "charily, with more than ordinary regard and tenderness."

19. *Lively.* To the life. Cf. *T. G. of V.* iv. 4. 174: "so lively :.cted ;" *T. of S.* ind. 2. 58: "As lively painted as the deed was done," etc.

26. *In thy not chiding.* A "little instance of tender remembrance in Leontes, which adds to the charming impression of Hermione's character" (Mrs. Jameson).

32. *As.* As *if.* See Gr. 107.

34. *Thus she stood*, etc. Mrs. Jameson remarks: "The expressions used here by Leontes, and by Polixenes [in 66 below], appear strangely applied to a statue, such as we usually imagine it—of the cold colourless marble ; but it is evident that in this scene Hermione personates one of those images or effigies, such as we may see in the old Gothic cathedrals, in which the stone, or marble, was coloured after nature. I remember coming suddenly upon one of these effigies, either at Basle or at Fribourg, which made me start : the figure was large as life ; the drapery of crimson, powdered with stars of gold ; the face and eyes and hair tinted after nature, though faded by time. It stood in a Gothic niche, over a tomb, as I think, and in a kind of dim uncertain light. It would have been very easy for a living person to represent such an effigy, particularly if it had been painted by that 'rare Italian master, Julio Romano,' who, as we are informed, was the reputed author of this wonderful statue."

That these painted statues were not unknown in the poet's time is evident from B. J., *Magnetic Lady*, v. 5 :

> "*Rut.* I 'd have her statue cut now in white marble.
> "*Sir Moth.* And have it painted in most orient colours.
> "*Rut.* That 's right! all city statues must be painted ;
> Else they 'll be worth nought in their subtle judgments."

The monumental bust of Shakespeare at Stratford was originally painted in imitation of nature, "the hands and face flesh colour, the eyes of a light hazel, the hair and beard auburn," etc. (Britton). Vasari states that Giulio Romano built a house for himself in Mantua, the front of which "he adorned with a fantastic decoration of coloured stuccoes."

42. *Standing like stone.* "The grief, the love, the remorse, and impatience of Leontes are finely contrasted with the astonishment and admiration of Perdita, who, gazing on the figure of her mother like one entranced, looks as if she were also turned to marble" (Mrs. Jameson).

56. *Piece up.* "Hoard up, so as to have his fill" (Schmidt).

58. *Wrought.* Wrought upon, agitated. Cf. *Temp.* iv. 1. 144:

> "your father 's in some passion
> That works him strongly;"

Id. v. 1. 17: "Your charm so strongly works 'em," etc. See also *Macb.* i. 3. 149 and *Oth.* v. 2. 345.

62. *Would I were dead*, etc. It has been suspected that a line is lost after this one; and the Coll. MS. inserts "I am but dead stone, looking upon stone." An anonymous conjecture (quoted by Sr.) is "I 'm in heaven, and looking on an angel." But, as Clarke remarks, the diction is in keeping with that of Leontes throughout—"disjointed, and full of sudden starts."

St. takes *Would I were dead but that*, etc., as = May I die if I do not think that already—she is alive, he would have said, had he not interrupted himself. But it is doubtful whether *but that* ever follows a clause of this kind, the simple *but* being regularly used.

67. *Fixure.* "Direction" (Schmidt). Edwards says: "The meaning is, though her eye be fixed (as the eye of a statue always is) yet it seems to have motion in it: that tremulous motion which is perceptible in the eye of a living person, how much soever one endeavour to fix it." In *T. and C.* i. 3. 101, the only other instance of the word in S., it is = stability. *Fixture* (= setting) occurs only in *M. W.* iii. 3. 67.

68. *As.* Changed by Capell to "and." Mason conjectures "so." Malone and Steevens take *as* to be = as if. Clarke explains it better: "Leontes refers to the contradiction in the first clause of his speech: The immobility of eye proper to a statue seems to have the motion of a living eye, as we are thus beguiled by art." *With* = by; as in v. 1. 113 and v. 2. 60 above.

86. *Resolve you.* Prepare yourselves.

96. *Unlawful business.* For the old laws against the practice of magical arts, see *A. Y. L.* p. 194, note on *Not damnable.*

100. *Look upon.* See on iv. 4. 435 above.

107. *Double.* For the adverbial use, cf. *A. W.* ii. 3. 254, *Macb.* i. 6. 15, iv. 1. 83, etc.

109. *Is she become the suitor?* Rowe changed the interrogation mark of the folio to a period, and has been generally followed, except by K. V., and the Camb. editors. We do not see much to choose between the readings, but on the whole prefer the old one. Paulina says in substance: Do not be afraid of her, but give her your hand; you wooed her once, is she become the suitor now? This does not imply that Hermione makes no advances, but rather indicates surprise that he who once wooed her should now "shun" her when she approaches him and let her do *all* the wooing.

111. *She embraces him.* On the silence of Hermione, see pp. 27 and 32 above.

122. *Your sacred vials.* Malone remarks that the expression seems to have been suggested by *Rev.* xvi. 1; and Halliwell adds *Isa.* xlv. 8.

129. *Push.* Impulse (Schmidt), or suggestion. Clarke explains it as "emergency, special occasion."

131. *You precious winners.* You who have gained what is precious to you.

132. *Partake.* Impart. Cf. *Per.* i. 1. 153 :

> "our mind partakes
> Her private actions to your secrecy."

Turtle. See on iv. 4. 154 above.

144. *Whose.* Referring to *Camillo,* not to *her.*

145. *Is richly noted.* The Var. of 1821 misprints "It richly noted." *Justified*=avouched. Cf. v. 2. 62 above.

147. *What! look upon my brother.* "How exquisitely this serves to depict the sensitively averted face of Hermione from Polixenes, recollecting all the misconstruction that had formerly grown out of her purely gracious attentions to him ; and also how sufficingly it shows the sincere repentance of Leontes for bygone errors, that he has had sixteen years to mourn and see in their true light ! No one better than Shakespeare knew the nobleness of a candid avowal of previous mistake, the relief of heart to its speaker, the elevated satisfaction to its hearers ; and with this crowning satisfaction he leaves us at the close of this grandly beautiful play" (Clarke).

148. *Holy.* Blameless. Cf. v. 1. 29, 31, and 169 above.

149. *This is your son-in-law,* etc. The folio reads thus :

> "This your Son-in-law,
> And Sonne vnto the King, whom heauens directing
> Is troth-plight to your daughter."

D. adopts Walker's suggestion of "This' your"="This is your," which, as the latter remarks, would not mar the metre, though he prefers the other. The "Globe" ed. inserts the "is." It seems awkward to make the leading sentence "This your son-in-law is troth-plight to your daughter"—the assertion being already implied in the subject—and to make "whom heavens directing" merely parenthetical. What Leontes says is rather, we think, "This *is* your son-in-law, and by heaven's direction he is troth-plight," etc. "Whom heavens directing" is a "confusion of construction" for "Who, heavens directing him." For many somewhat similar ones, see Gr. 249, 410, and 415. Capell changed *whom* to "who," as the "Globe" ed. does.

For *troth-plight,* cf. *Hen. V.* ii. 1. 21 : "you were troth-plight to her."

ADDENDA.

THE ILLUSTRATIONS.—As we are unable to give pictorial illustrations of Shakespeare's Bohemia (except the one on page 9, to which we venture to say no other "local habitation" can be assigned), we insert a few that belong to the real Bohemia of that day. The royal palace and the cathedral at Prague were old buildings even then ; but the portal to the former (see p. 41) was designed by Scamozzi, and the royal mausoleum in the latter (p. 8) was the work of Colin of Malines, both of whom were contemporaries of the poet.

THE "TIME-ANALYSIS" OF THE PLAY.—We give below the summing-up of Mr. P. A. Daniel's "time-analysis" in his paper "On the Times or Durations of the Action of Shakspere's Plays" (*Trans. of New Shaks. Soc.* 1877–79, p. 177), with a few explanatory extracts from the preceding pages appended as foot-notes:

"The time of this Play comprises eight days represented on the stage; with intervals.

Day 1. Act I. sc. i. and ii.
" 2. Act II. sc. i.*
    An Interval of twenty-three days.†
" 3. Act II. sc. ii. and iii., and Act III. sc. i.
" 4. Act III. sc. ii.
    An Interval. Antigonus's voyage to Bohemia.
" 5. Act III. sc. iii.
    An Interval (Act IV. sc. i.) of sixteen years.‡
" 6. Act IV. sc. ii. and iii.§
" 7. Act IV. sc. iv.
    An Interval. The journey to Sicilia.
" 8. Act V. sc. i.–iii."

LIST OF CHARACTERS IN THE PLAY, WITH THE SCENES IN WHICH THEY APPEAR.—The numbers in parentheses indicate the lines the characters have in each scene.

Leontes: i. 2(210); ii. 1(108), 3(109); iii. 2(73); v. 1(105), 3(76). Whole no. 681.
  Mamillius: i. 2(4); ii. 1(18). Whole no. 22.
  Camillo: i. 1(26), 2(123); iv. 2(18), 4(131); v. 3(7). Whole no. 305.
  Antigonus: ii. 1(30), 3(29); iii. 3(51). Whole no. 110.
  Cleomenes: iii. 1(11), 2(1); v. 1(12). Whole no. 24.
  Dion: iii. 1(16), 2(1); v. 1(11). Whole no. 28.
  Polixenes: i. 2(129); iv. 2(44), 4(94); v. 3(10). Whole no. 277.
  Florizel: iv. 4(167); v. 1(38). Whole no. 205.
  Archidamus: i. 1(24). Whole no. 24.
  Shepherd: iii. 3(47); iv. 4(89); v. 2(8). Whole no. 144.

---

* "I am not sure that a separate day should be given to this scene; but, on the whole, the proposed departure of Polixenes and Camillo on the *night* of the first day, and the mission, *since then*, of Cleomenes and Dion to Delphos make this division probable."

† "'*Twenty-three days*,' says Leontes, 'they have been absent: 't is good speed,' etc.; and he orders a session to be summoned for the arraignment of the queen."

‡ "Note that Camillo makes his absence from Sicilia to be *fifteen* years. This is probably a mere error of the printer or copyist. Besides the *sixteen* announced by Time, the Chorus, *sixteen* years is the period again twice mentioned in act v. sc. iii.—line 31, 'Which lets go by some *sixteen* years;' and line 50, 'Which *sixteen* winters cannot blow away,' etc."

§ "Autolycus cheats the Clown (the Shepherd's son) of his purse as he is on his way to buy things for the sheep-shearing festival. This incident suggests the placing of the festival on the following day."

Clown: iii. 3(38) ; iv. 3(48), 4(86) ; v. 2(37). Whole no. 209.
Autolycus: iv. 3(87), 4(207) ; v. 2(25). Whole no. 319.
Mariner: iii. 3(11). Whole no. 11.
Gaoler: ii. 2(13). Whole no. 13.
Officer: iii. 2(27), Whole no. 27.
1st Lord: ii. 1(18), 3(12) ; iii. 2(9) ; v. 1(24). Whole no. 63.
1st Gentleman: v. 1(18), 2(30). Whole no. 48.
2d Gentleman: v. 2(17). Whole no. 17.
3d Gentleman: v. 2(71). Whole no. 71.
1st Servant: ii. 3(8) ; iii. 2(5) ; iv. 4(39). Whole no. 52.
2d Servant: ii. 3(2). Whole no. 2.
Time (Chorus): iv. 1(32). Whole no. 32.
Hermione: i. 2(68) ; ii. 1(46) ; iii. 2(89) ; v. 3(8). Whole no. 211.
Perdita: iv. 4(118) ; v. 1(3), 3(7). Whole no. 128.
Paulina: ii. 2(44), 3(84) ; iii. 2(60) ; v. 1(67), 3(76). Whole no. 331.
Emilia: ii. 2(20). Whole no. 20.
Mopsa: iv. 4(21). Whole no. 21.
Dorcas: iv. 4(13). Whole no. 13.
1st Lady: ii. 1(9). Whole no. 9.
2d Lady: ii. 1(4). Whole no. 4.

In the above enumeration, parts of lines are counted as whole lines, making the total in the play greater than it is. The actual number of lines in each scene (Globe edition numbering) is as follows : i. 1(50), 2(465) ; ii. 1(199), 2(66), 3(207) ; iii. 1(22), 2(244), 3(143) ; iv. 1(32), 2(62), 3(135), 4(873) ; v. 1(233), 2(188), 3(155). Whole number in the play, 3074.

INDEX OF WORDS AND PHRASES EXPLAINED.

On source material, Hermione when charged
with adultery, fell on her knees + begged Leontes
to send to the oracle for proof.

Shakespeare has the king send — because
when he disbelieves the oracles answer that
Hermione is innocent. Disbelief of oracle
is disbelief of gods — hence blasphemy